HISTORY OF
Lovespoons

HISTORY OF *Lovespoons*

The Art and Traditions of a Romantic Craft

David Western

FOX CHAPEL
PUBLISHING

ISBN 978-1-56523-673-8

Library of Congress Cataloging-in-Publication Data

Western, David H., 1960-

History of lovespoons / David Western.

    p. cm.

Includes index.

ISBN 978-1-56523-673-8

1. Love spoons. I. Title.

GT2950.W47 2012

745.51--dc23

           2011030981

To learn more about the other great books from Fox Chapel Publishing, or to find a retailer near you, call toll-free 800-457-9112 or visit us at www.FoxChapelPublishing.com.

Note to Authors: We are always looking for talented authors to write new books in our area of woodworking, design, and related crafts. Please send a brief letter describing your idea to Acquisition Editor, 1970 Broad Street, East Petersburg, PA 17520.

Printed in Indonesia
First printing

Preface

One of the finest lovespoon carvers of his generation, author David Western is also an authority on the origins and development of a tradition that has thrilled and delighted for many centuries.

This publication is an illuminating and immensely readable source examining the story of the lovespoon, from its early days as a token of affection, to the exquisitely produced examples commissioned today as gifts for special occasions.

The author examines the lovespoon from an international perspective, challenging the many myths that continue to surround it and assessing the changing direction of the craft over time. He also considers the spoons from a technical viewpoint by commenting on the diversity of designs and carving techniques of both historical and contemporary examples.

There can be no one more passionate about the lovespoon than David Western, and this informative and extremely well-researched book will undoubtedly appeal to all those who share his enthusiasm for such a fascinating subject.

Dr. Emma Lile
Curator: Social and Cultural History
St. Fagans National History Museum of Wales
Cardiff, Wales

Acknowledgments

Very little historical information exists on folk art in general, and on lovespoons
particular, making the advice and guidance of experts in the field invaluable in compil
this book.

I would especially like to thank Dr. Herbert E. Roese, author of the thought provok
article, *Lovespoons in Perspective*, for his tireless help tracking down items
lovespoon esoterica and for his convincing arguments concerning the origins a
purposes of the lovespoon. Without Herbert's enthusiastic support, I would never h
realized how broad and interesting the field of lovespoon history is.

Emma Lile and Meinwen Ruddock at St. Fagans National History Museum of Wa
have offered this project tremendously generous support. From supplying histori
photographs to critiquing the manuscript and providing the book's preface, their h
has been invaluable and is greatly appreciated.

Discovering the depth of Scandinavian lovespoon carving has been a wonderful surp
of my research, but I would not have found nearly as much material without the genero
help of Maria Perers and Marie Tornehave at the Nordiska Museet, Stockholm, and Jol
Knuttson at the Linköping University's Carl Malmsten Furniture Studies Departme
Janike Ugelstad and Kari Bjorg Vold Halvorsen at the Norsk Folkemuseum, Oslo, patier
answered my many questions about the Norwegian lovespoon tradition and supplied
with access to a wealth of historical photographs.

Thanks to Michael Freeman at the Ceredigion Museum, Aberystwyth, who generou
allowed me to use photographs of spoons from their wonderful collection. I would also like
thank Bianca Slowik at the Germanisches Nationalmuseum, Nuremberg, for her assista
in tracking down the elusive 1664 lovespoon.

Many thanks to lovespoon carvers Alun Davies, Mike Davies, Laura Jenkins Gor
Ralph Hentall, Adam King, Siôn Llewellyn, and David Stanley, who very kindly allowed
to use photographs of their work and offered great support during the writing process, a
to Judy Ritger, who supplied me with photos of her beautiful kolrosing work.

A special thanks to Nola, who made this all possible.

Finally, I would like to thank my father Charles for his elegant lovespoon sketches a
Chris Roberts for his remarkably beautiful photography. Every picture truly does tell a sto

Ginny's Butterflies, David Western, spalted and figured birch, 2010. A cloud of butterflies emerges from a field of flowers on this wedding spoon. The highly figured grain of the spalted birch brings colorful detail to the butterfly wings and some drama to the scene. 16" L by 6" W by ¾" D. Photo by Chris Roberts.

Introduction

Since at least the mid-seventeenth century, the lovespoon has been a pre-eminent messenger of love and romance. Long before bank-draining diamond rings and wallet-busting wedding dresses were the expectation, a young man would demonstrate his ardor, skill, and tenacity for the girl who had captivated him through a virtuoso display of woodcarving.

His extraordinary offering, often the result of months of laborious handwork aided only by the most basic tools, would undeniably indicate to his young lady the bottomless depth of his passion. It would also give her family clear proof of his skills and value as a worker and would demonstrate to all who viewed it that its recipient was desirable to suitors.

Although the Industrial Revolution, changing tastes, and the murderous savagery of the First World War all played a part in driving many types of folk art to extinction, the lovespoon still survives and is now even experiencing something of a revival.

In a cynical age of instant gratification and obsession with shallow style and celebrity taste, there is still a place for the lovespoon's unpretentious honesty. As long as human beings are capable of feeling love, the lovespoon remains a most reliable and relevant messenger through which to express it.

—David Western

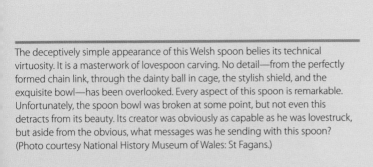

The deceptively simple appearance of this Welsh spoon belies its technical virtuosity. It is a masterwork of lovespoon carving. No detail—from the perfectly formed chain link, through the dainty ball in cage, the stylish shield, and the exquisite bowl—has been overlooked. Every aspect of this spoon is remarkable. Unfortunately, the spoon bowl was broken at some point, but not even this detracts from its beauty. Its creator was obviously as capable as he was lovestruck, but aside from the obvious, what messages was he sending with this spoon? (Photo courtesy National History Museum of Wales: St Fagans.)

Table of Contents

Learn about the cultural and artistic significance of lovespoons

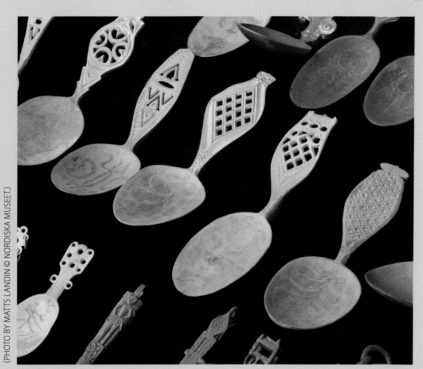

(PHOTO BY MATTS LANDIN © NORDISKA MUSEET)

(PHOTO COURTESY NATIONAL HISTORY MUSEUM OF WALES: ST FAGANS.)

The history See page 12

The origins See page 16

The types that exist See page 20

Experience the beauty of lovespoons with this gallery from today's finest carvers See page 76

(PHOTO COURTESY NATIONAL HISTORY MUSEUM OF WALES: ST FAGANS.)

The symbols that appear in lovespoons See page 32

The myths about lovespoons See page 28

How to interpret symbols used in lovespoons See page 46

CHAPTER 1
The History of Lovespoons

The lovespoon is the only one out of an array of richly ornamented wooden love tokens that has survived in a meaningful way into the modern era. During the early 1600s, it became common for young men to decorate utilitarian objects with elaborate romantic carving as gifts for the young unmarried women who had captured their hearts. These gifts, ranging from stay busks and knitting sheaths to mangle boards and washing bats, were carved throughout Europe. From Scandinavia to Romania, every area of the continent experienced this romantic folk tradition.

Although it reached its artistic zenith in Wales and Sweden, the carving of wooden spoons was a popular tradition throughout the European continent. The rural farming classes primarily carved the spoons, although it was also common for sailors to engage in the practice. Later, professional carvers became involved, but initially lovespoon carving was very much an amateur endeavor.

(Left) Many types of wooden love tokens were created during the period of approximately 1600–1900. All were lavishly and expressively carved, demonstrating both fervent passion and technical skill. These stay busks were worn as ribbing in a woman's dress and gave her torso the rigid support that was the style of the day. Since they were worn next to the body, their romantic symbolism was not lost on love-struck young carvers!
(Right) Welsh lovespoon carving was stylistically and symbolically diverse. Historical examples are rich in variety and exuberant detailing. (Photo courtesy National History Museum of Wales: St Fagans.)

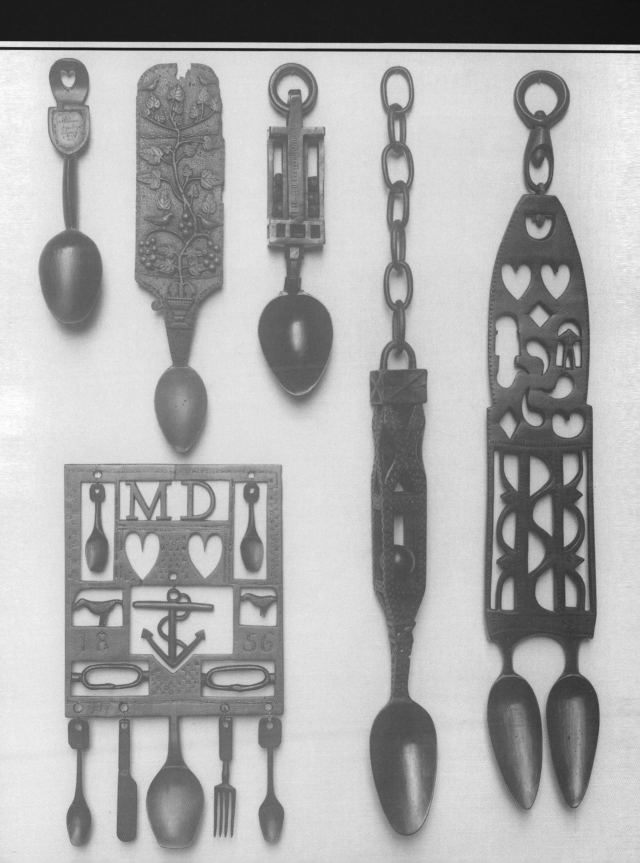

NEW PURPOSE

This vibrant tradition has undergone a transformation in recent years, with lovespoons seldom being carved for their original purpose of initiating relationships. In contrast to the old tradition, today's spoons are more often carved to celebrate important occasions such as weddings and anniversaries, which occur *after* the establishment of a relationship. However, many of those just discovering the tradition are under the impression that the woeful souvenir and gift shop spoons shown on many Internet sites represent what lovespoon carving is all about. Nothing could be further from the truth. Lovespoon carving is as much about emotion as it is about manual dexterity, and modern commercial spoons are almost completely lacking in any sort of passion or sentiment. Historically, the carvers would throw themselves into the task with abandon and would do everything they could to create a beautiful spoon with their personal imprint on it, no matter what their skill level. Studying antique examples clearly illustrates this point; the old spoons have a liveliness and vibrancy that is entirely missing from most modern mass-produced commercial spoons.

The history of this tradition, like that of so many folk arts, is shrouded in mystery. Perhaps, because it was primarily a craft of the rural poor, the practices and purposes behind this tradition were not considered particularly important or interesting, so little was ever written about it, and much has been left to supposition and conjecture.

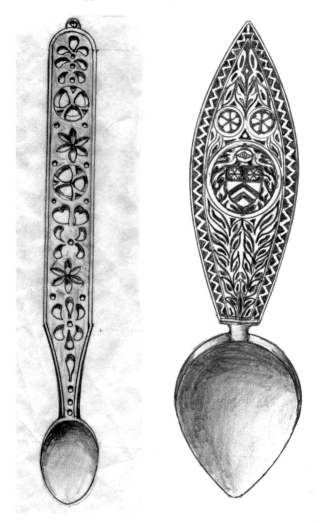

Young shepherds would often while away long hours carving elaborate lovespoons for the young girls who had captivated them. The carvers of the Alentejo region of Portugal were particularly renowned for their carving skills. (Drawing courtesy of Charles Western.)

THE BEGINNING

Precisely why the humble spoon became such a romantic symbol is unknown, but several dated examples help tell us *when* the spoon-carving tradition began. We can be relatively certain it occurred mid-seventeenth century, around the same time it became more common to decorate and present other wooden utilitarian objects as gifts. At this time, the explosion of art and culture, which had worked its way northward from Italy and downward from the nobility, reached the masses. Throughout Europe, the standard of living of the poorest citizens (primarily those living in rural areas who still made up the majority of the population) improved slightly, allowing folk art to flourish. One way this development manifested itself was people no longer had to spend all their time engaged in survival-based work. With free time now available to them, young men were able to decorate some of the plain wooden household objects they and their families had made for utilitarian use, and young women were able to begin beautifying their textile products.

With limited access to tools and only the most basic materials at hand, young carvers could have been content with simplicity; but fortified by love and devotion, the results of their labors often reached a level of artistic sophistication and craftsmanship far in excess of what we might expect. Unfortunately, dated spoons (page 17) are uncommon. Time and dates were simply not as important to the rural folk of seventeenth-century Europe as they are today and few carvers seemed to have felt dating their handiwork was an important consideration.

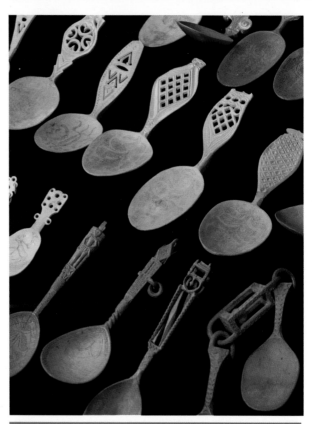

The lovespoon tradition in Sweden was a long and vibrant one. The spoons were invariably of high-quality craftsmanship, but the designs and symbols were somewhat more conservative than those found in Welsh spooncarving. (Photo by Matts Landin © Nordiska Museet)

Fretted work became more refined and delicate as tool quality improved and as the challenge of surpassing previous spoons became more daunting. A fine example of gorgeous pierced work and tracery, this spoon is a marvelous example of a broad panel. Despite being large, the spoon appears extremely delicate due to the repetition of the pointed arches running along its edges and the remarkable circular tracery in its middle section. The work of a sure hand, this spoon shows us Welsh lovespoon carving at its graceful best. Sadly, it has been broken and rather clumsily repaired, appearing to result in the loss of a crown detail. (Photo courtesy Ceredigion Museum, Aberystwyth Wales.)

Origins of romantic spoon carving

The practice of romantic spoon carving and giving seems to have developed from approximately the mid-1600s. Possibly the oldest dated lovespoon is one held in the collections of the Germanisches National Museum, Nuremberg. Dated 1664, it is an example of a "couple spoon." Richly carved, the spoon features an embracing couple on its rat-tailed (or spiked) handle. Its lack of wear indicates it has been well cared for over the centuries and was not created for a utilitarian purpose.

The oldest Welsh lovespoon, dating from 1667, is of a completely different style. Although more robust stylistically and physically than its German counterpart, this spoon does show off a number of subtle features. A pair of elegant cages houses a number of carefully crafted rolling balls and the spoon's crown is finished with delicate chip-carved patterning.

A spoon from 1657 that is housed in the Nordiska Museet along with one dated 1654 that is housed in the collection of the Museum of European Civilization in Marseille, France, may well also be contenders for the title of oldest dated lovespoon. Elegant detailing and lack of wear hints these spoons were not made for everyday use. However, the religious imagery and lack of romantic symbolism found on the Swedish spoon would suggest it perhaps had a religious rather than romantic purpose. The Breton spoon is decorated with an engraved date and the family name Coz and is highly ornamented with a variety of carving. Whether it was given as a romantic gift is not known at this time.

Couple spoon carved from boxwood, in 1664. (Photo courtesy Germanisches National Museum, Nuremberg.)

Welsh lovespoon carved from sycamore in 1667. (Photo courtesy National History Museum of Wales: St Fagans)

'WHY' AND 'HOW'

A number of theories have been advanced to explain *why* and *how* the lovespoon developed. One suggestion is the spoon was chosen as a love token due to its association with sustenance and its symbolic link to the nurturing of body and soul. I think this is likely to be an excessively romantic notion. At the time of the lovespoon's inception, spoons were not used a great deal by the rural classes for eating. While the upper classes had begun using metal spoons for dining on soups and stews, the rural folk still primarily drank and ate directly from the bowl.

Most romantic tokens were the result of utilitarian objects being heavily ornamented, and the lovespoon is no different. Probably the most prevalent theory, especially in Wales, where the craft remains at its strongest, is the lovespoon developed from *cawl* spoons and ladles, which were used to prepare and serve this staple Welsh stew. While a conceivable theory for Wales, it does not explain the development of the lovespoon in countries where stew or soup was not a main culinary feature.

It also does not explain why lovespoons bear so little resemblance to cawl spoons.

Dated lovespoons are uncommon, though there are some examples, like this spoon from 1727. (Photo courtesy National History Museum of Wales: St Fagans.)

Spooning

The once popular expression, *spooning,* to indicate the somewhat frivolous and sentimental canoodling that accompanies a romantic courtship, is thought to have arisen due to the popularity of lovespoon carving. In South Wales, the term was very common, and a young woman's suitor was often referred to as her *spooner*. Other European countries in which spoon carving was common also share similar expressions for this type of courtship activity. Today, the expression refers more to an act of cuddling and its roots in romantic spoon carving have been largely forgotten.

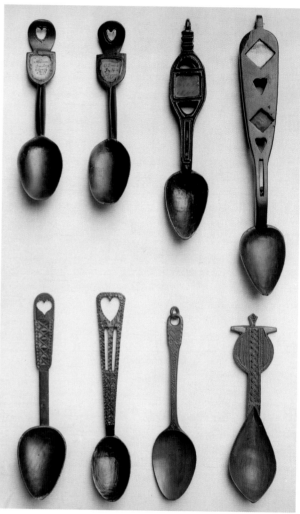

This collection of spoons dramatically illustrates the egg-shaped bowl, which was far more common to the metal spoon than to the broader and more circular shape of the cawl spoon. The only exception is the oddly shaped spoon in the bottom right corner, which is possibly of African origin, its dramatic bowl being of a style common to areas of that continent. (Photos courtesy National History Museum of Wales: St Fagans.)

Very few historical Welsh lovespoons have the distinctive round bowl of the cawl spoon. Almost all have the more egg-shaped bowl of the metal spoon.

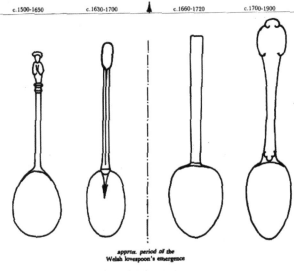

c.1500-1650   c.1630-1700   c.1660-1720   c.1700-1900

approx. period of the
Welsh lovespoon's emergence

Fig. 1: Schematised development of spoon shapes.

The predominantly egg-shaped bowl of historical lovespoons would indicate the origin of the craft took place around the mid-seventeenth century, in concert with the development and acceptance of that style on metal spoons. Before this, most spoon bowls followed a shape almost the reverse of what we now consider standard. On medieval spoons, the bowl commonly narrows at the handle and widens toward the end—a shape rarely seen on lovespoons and bridal spoons. (Diagram courtesy of Dr. H.E. Roese)

BOWL SHAPE

The bowl shape of nearly every historical Welsh lovespoon in museums and private collections is consistent with the bowl shape of metal spoons. The rounded bowl of the cawl spoon is present on less than five percent of historical examples. Even the earliest Welsh lovespoon has the classic egg-shaped bowl of the metal spoon. This bowl shape coincides with the development of the metal dining spoon, which had found favor among the upper classes of society and would seem to indicate a desire among the rural poor to mimic that style in wood. Many spoons in the Swedish and Norwegian collections show a remarkable similarity to prevalent metal designs of the time and it seems very likely that imitation was the inspiration for the lovespoon.

With many rural girls working for the gentry as scullery maids and cooks and the necessity for the upper classes to display their wealth as a status indicator, it is very conceivable that silver spoons and their accompanying cachet were well known among the poorer classes.

As years passed and the tradition became more popular, the heavily ornamented, decorative spoon we know today as the lovespoon evolved, probably as a result of changing tastes, improved tools, and successive generations of carvers striving to outdo what had come before them.

SIMILAR TRAITS

Despite primarily being made by rural folk of limited financial means who rarely journeyed more than a few miles from home, lovespoons from Wales and Sweden to the far reaches of the European continent share several similar traits. The use of simple chip-carving techniques, geometric patterns, and various romantic symbols are common to spoons carved throughout Europe. As with Welsh spoons, it seems to have been the trend among continental European lovespoon carvers, that no matter how complex the design, each individual spoon would be carved from a single piece of wood.

Over the years, it has become a tradition and point of pride that a lovespoon always be carved in this way. The idea of gluing sections together is frowned upon and now tends to be viewed with contempt by most modern lovespoon carvers. With the advent of ever more affordable tools, carvers throughout Britain and Europe were able to make use of fine saws, gouges, files, and planes to undertake increasingly more difficult carvings. Many spoons from Wales and the European continent dating from the late 1800s demonstrate a wider handle panel and ornate fretted (saw-cut) patterning. This nineteenth-century *gingerbread* style, made possible by these newly affordable tools, became the rage in many areas of woodworking at that time.

These fretted spoons, carved in Sweden during the mid-nineteenth century from what is likely birch, are strikingly similar to spoons carved in Wales during the same period and illustrate the type of fretted designs that were all the rage at that time. (Photo by Sören Hallgren ©Nordiska Museet.)

COINCIDENTAL DEVELOPMENT

Regardless of these similarities, it is highly unlikely that many of the young men carving lovespoons during the early years of the tradition were exposed in any great manner to the wood carving of foreigners. Much of the evolution of the lovespoon throughout so many far-flung countries is likely to be a case of coincidental development, which makes it virtually impossible to conclude *who* was responsible for the creation of lovespoon carving.

CATEGORIES

Lovespoons seem to fall into several classification categories, depending on the cultural traditions present in the country of their creation.

TESTER SPOONS

In Sweden, many spoons were considered *feeler* or *tester* gifts and were given by a boy to one or more girls to gauge what type of return interest the spoons would generate. Often, these spoons lacked the intense workmanship and fervent passion found in spoons carved with more serious intent. Sometimes, the young men would sport these spoons, worn visible from the breast pocket, as a well-known way for them to show romantic intent when calling on their young ladies (Knutsson).

Front and side view: Simple but lovingly crafted spoons like these were a good way for a young man to determine if the young woman who had captured his heart felt the same way in return. Left and middle spoon are 10" L by 2" W by ¾" D. Spoon at right is 8" L by 3" W by ¾" D. (Photos by Chris Roberts.)

FEELER SPOONS

In Hungary, similar spoons are said to have been exchanged by young suitors at a yearly festival known as *bucsu* (pronounced boo-choo), where the idea of *feeler* was apparently taken to another level. Elaborately designed spoons were purchased and further decorated by young men who would give them to girls they had fallen for, with acceptance of the spoon indicating a mutual interest. However, young men who did not have a particular girl in mind would also buy spoons and offer them as gifts to girls who happened to catch their eye. If the girl refused the gift, the young man would smack her bottom with it. Apparently, the rejected young men could sometimes get carried away with the bottom smacking and many of the prettiest girls who were not interested in becoming attached went home with very sore backsides!

LOVESPOONS

In Wales and many parts of Europe, it seems lovespoons were given with a more serious intent. Judging by the amount of labor, time, and effort that most certainly went into most of them, these spoons might conceivably have been given when a positive response from the young lady was more of a possibility. These spoons were not considered a betrothal gift or a binding marriage contract; their acceptance by the young lady would most likely have merely been a green light for a more formal courtship to begin, but they did represent a serious commitment of time and emotion by the carver, and a rejection would have been a devastating disappointment.

Spoons of this type are the ones most often found in museum and private collections and are the type we commonly associate with the term lovespoon today. The

It is impossible to tell if this elegant spoon is the work of an assured amateur or that of a professional, but it is notable for its delicacy and for the wax inlay applied to the engraved initials and date. The oddly shaped bowl is likely the result of the spoon's fall from its place on a wall, landing on the tip of the bowl, and chipping it off. This spoon has been simply repaired by squaring the broken section of the bowl end. Sadly, the fine tracery from the crown portion of the spoon has been lost, so we can only guess at the form it took. A number of comma-shaped "soul" symbols are fretted through this spoon with a very fine border of chip carving to complete this very expert design. (Photo courtesy National History Museum of Wales: St Fagans.)

young man himself generally carved these spoons, although it appears that later, professionals (most likely trained carvers or cabinetmakers) were occasionally hired to carry out the work if the young swain was not particularly handy with the necessary tools. In some countries, the hiring of professionals to carve love tokens took on a dual purpose. The professional provided a better quality product and the ability to afford the cost of his services gave both the giver and the recipient of the gift increased social prestige.

WEDDING SPOONS

A third type of spoon, which appears throughout Europe and many other areas of the world, is the wedding spoon. While not considered lovespoons in the narrowest sense of the definition, that is to say, a gift to initiate a relationship, these spoons are still an important part of the romantic spoon tradition.

Commonly appearing at the wedding celebration or as part of the wedding dowry, spoons of this type did not appear during the courtship phase as statements of love or romantic interest. Often their purpose would be to indicate a level of prosperity or standing (the notion of what constituted prosperity being vastly different in rural seventeenth-century Europe to what it is in modern Europe or North America), or to illustrate the bride's desirability. Wedding spoons could be used for symbolic effect. Spoons such as the double spoon, joined by chain link and commonly found in Norway, were typically used at the marriage ceremony or supper to show the couple was now united as one.

When used in this manner, the chain would be draped over the bride and bridegroom's shoulders, with each having a spoon. Sometimes they would each use an end of the spoon to eat their first meal, the chain symbolically linking their hands as they ate. In Brittany, the groom would often wear a unique folding spoon in his hatband or belt during the marriage festivities, and guests attending the wedding feast often wore lovespoons hung from their waistcoat buttons.

A Breton folding spoon with a metal hinge pin. (Photo courtesy National History Museum of Wales: St Fagans.)

Richly carved and deeply symbolic, the Norwegian bridal spoon represented the union of two souls at marriage. On the second or third wedding day, the couple would eat a meal of bridal porridge together using the spoon. Led by a fiddle player, several women carrying bowls of porridge would follow the bride to the table where the couple would use the spoon to eat a ritual meal together. The purpose of this ceremony was to illustrate the bride's new status as a housewife. Carved from birch, the spoon is 26" L by 3½" W by 1" D. Carved by the author in 2010. (Photo by Chris Roberts.)

Swedish *Gycklarsked* (jokespoons)

A number of unusual Swedish wedding spoons were carved for use by the bride and groom at their ceremonies or wedding meals. These spoons often featured a bowl at each end of the handle, frequently with one upside-down of the other. Other jokespoons included single-bowl spoons with the bowl upside down and set at ninety degrees from the handle, or multi-bowled spoons with the bowls protruding at odd angles from the handle. To the great entertainment of the guests, the wedding couple would use the jokespoon to attempt eating together at the wedding feast or at their first meal together. The three spoons were carved by the author. The spoons dimensions are, from left: 12" L by 2.5" W by 3"D, 11" L by 1½" W by ¾" D, and 7" L by 1½" W by ½" D.

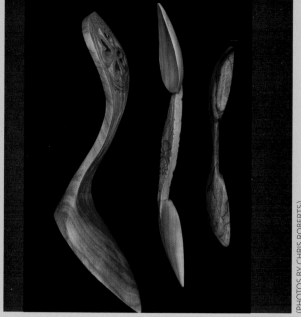

DECLINE

The fortunes of the lovespoon suffered a decline at the end of the nineteenth century and worsened again during the early years of the twentieth century. Throughout Wales and Europe, there was rapid social change. The Industrial Revolution brought cheap materials to the markets and consumers demanded products of greater sophistication than rural craftsmen produced.

Tastes had turned away from handcrafted wooden gifts as gold rings and diamonds became the new standard for engagement and wedding gifts. Combined with mass migration from the country to new industrial cities, the balance of country life had been irreversibly altered. The mass carnage of two world wars then effectively ended the three hundred year tradition of most rural wooden folk arts by stealing almost entire generations of the young craftsmen who would have been making them.

TRADITION HANGS ON

However, as other crafts disappeared forever, the lovespoon tradition tenaciously hung on. Continued by a few amateur carvers working from tiny villages and farmsteads in rural Wales, the convention persisted much as it had for centuries. Although it became uncommon for lovespoons to be given as love tokens by hopeful suitors, they began being given instead as engagement or wedding gifts.

From around the 1950s onward, a number of craftsmen began carving spoons for a wider range of occasions, including birthdays and anniversaries. It also became popular for spoons to be presented at formal occasions as symbolic gifts of Wales. These presentation-style spoons tended to be heavier on nationalist or commercial sentiment than they were on romance, indicating a subtle change in their purpose.

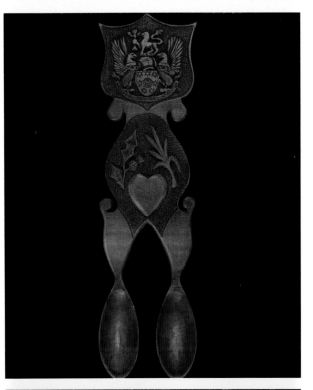

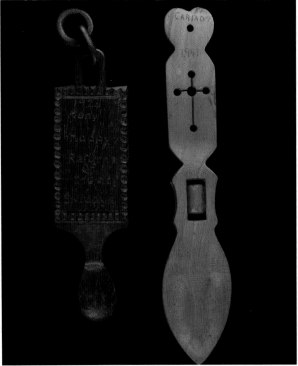

(Top) Welsh lovespoons began to be given at a wider range of occasions during the latter half of the twentieth century. This period saw the birth of the "presentation" type of lovespoon, such as this one, carved by Brindley Roberts for the BBC in 1956.

(Bottom) In the early to middle part of the twentieth century, few lovespoons were carved. Those that were, like these spoons, tended to be very simple and although touching, seem to lack some of the passion and technical skill of older spoons. (Photos by Chris Roberts.)

TOURISM BRINGS RESURGENCE

The 1960s and beyond witnessed the remarkable growth of world tourism, and with it, an explosive development of the lovespoon as a large turnover souvenir item. This has, however, been something of a double-edged sword. On one hand, the mass production of simple, economically priced lovespoons has brought the tradition to the attention of millions of tourists who have taken them home as impulse purchases. On the other hand, in comparison with handmade artifacts, commercially run operations often lead to a drop in quality. Mass production has created an expectation of cheapness, which has degraded both the quality of the designs and the craftsmanship involved in making modern lovespoons.

Fortunately, many amateur carvers continue the older traditions by producing unique handcarved lovespoons for their family or friends. In some respects, this mirrors the old days when the individuals carving spoons were motivated more by emotion than by a commercial interest. This is a positive thing, because it allows the craft to grow and profit from a variety of experiences and backgrounds, free of the constraints of the commercial market.

Although mass-produced spoons are economically priced for quick sale, they lack the beauty, technical skill, and most important, the strong emotional feel of individually handcrafted spoons. (Photo by Chris Roberts.)

Narrow and paneled spoons

As lovespoon carving evolved, the designs became increasingly complicated and competitive. To accommodate the extra carving "activity," carvers began expanding the width and length of the handles. The panel handle rapidly became very popular among Welsh carvers, with some taking them to great extremes as is shown by these examples. These behemoths must have been carved from impressive timbers, but despite their massive and brawny appearance, they are very finely carved. The curious pierced symbols have an almost hieroglyphic feel and are arranged in total symmetry. Although some of the symbols are quickly recognizable, such as the hearts, soul symbols, diamonds, and keyholes, many are simply baffling. Whether or not they were secretly understood between the carver and his beloved is unknown; they certainly are fascinating. The mighty rings connecting the panels indicate that the original timber from which these spoons were carved would have been substantially thick, as do the deeply hollowed triangular bowls.

Although broad-paneled spoons became a popular way for carvers to demonstrate their skill, narrow-handled spoons were equally popular. Many historical examples seem to be conscious efforts to mimic the ornate handles of the fine silver and metal spoons used by the aristocracy. This dazzling example is notable not only for its craftsmanship, but for the unique nut that slides over the octagonal stem. It also has a gorgeously carved heart-shaped bowl, a feature surprisingly rare among historical examples. The rectangular handle is sparsely decorated with a refined chip-carved pattern and holds both a rolling ball and a swivel arrangement. Superbly crafted and proportioned, the spoon was likely carved by a woodworker with some experience. Despite the restraint of its design, this is a very powerful spoon. (Photo courtesy National History Museum of Wales: St Fagans.)

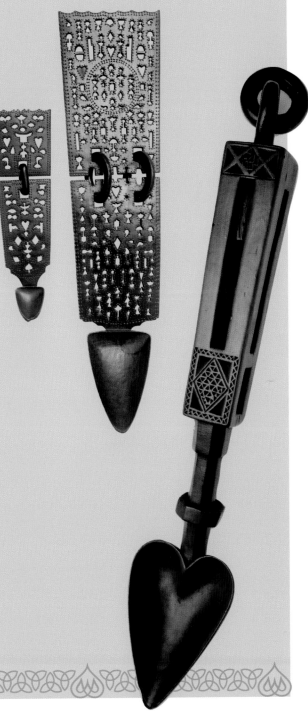

CHAPTER 2
Lovespoon Myths

A number of myths and symbols have accompanied the lovespoon into the twenty-first century. Most notable among them is the notion that the acceptance of such a spoon indicated a binding betrothal agreement. There is no documented evidence that this was ever the case. Indeed, it seems more likely that the giving and acceptance of a lovespoon was simply the precursor to the beginning of a relationship. Carving a lovespoon was an excellent way for a young man to indicate his desire, showcase his manual skills, and gauge any reciprocal interest he might receive from the recipient of his gift.

Celtic Cinnamon Buns, David Western, red alder, 2010. The title says it all! 17" L by 4½" W by ¾" D. (Photo by Chris Roberts.)

NOT A CELTIC TRADITION

Another misconception is the notion that lovespoons are a Celtic tradition. There is a Celtic aspect to it in the sense that the Welsh are Celts, but curiously, the lovespoon's influence did not spread to Ireland, Scotland, the Isle of Man, Cornwall, or Galicia in any appreciable way. In the British Isles, few spoons have been collected from outside Wales, indicating a tradition that was quite localized. In Brittany, a vibrant spoon carving culture was renowned for the elegant folding marriage spoon worn in the belt or hatband by the groom on his wedding day. Bretons were also proud of wearing ornately carved spoons hung from a waistcoat button while attending celebrations or feasts. However, it seems that in Brittany, romantic spoons tended to be presented at weddings rather than used to initiate a relationship as was common with the Welsh and Swedish spoons.

In most of the other Celtic nations, the pastime is little known, and scant evidence exists to support the notion lovespoon carving was ever an appreciable part of their traditions. Today, Celtic knotwork and crosses are common features of many lovespoon designs. The complicated patterns, especially endless knots, have become a symbol of eternity. Celtic knotwork lends the lovespoon a delicacy and sophistication that would have been almost impossible for carvers to achieve before the advent of thin saw blades and needle files, but it is important to note that Celtic imagery or knotwork is virtually unknown on historical samples.

NOT UNIQUE TO WALES

A common advertising statement seen on Internet business and cultural websites suggests lovespoon carving is unique to Wales and that the tradition originated there. While the large number of lovespoons found throughout many European countries easily disproves the first part of the statement, deciding who began the tradition is an altogether tougher proposition. The likelihood that one country originated the idea and all others followed after is a slim one at best. Like most arts, very little occurs in a vacuum and judging by its vast spread, the folk arts of seventeenth-century Europe were developing in many locations at the same time.

There has been some suggestion that Welsh lovespoons can be identified by region and that various areas of Wales

Celtic knotwork is a recent feature in lovespoon carving. (Photo by Chris Roberts.)

had distinct techniques that were employed when a spoon was carved.

SPOON SIMILARITIES

Similarities do exist in spoons from particular areas, such as those with small glass panels or dolphin-shaped ridged handles that originated in the Caernarfon area, or the twin-panel spoon common to Pembroke.

However, these details appear on spoons from other areas of Wales as well and do not exist in large enough numbers in the home region to constitute definitive proof of a local style. It is most likely that young carvers worked to the best of their abilities; some would have been inspired by examples they may have seen locally, but others would have made up their own designs as they carved. The spoons found in many museum collections were often gathered without their provenance, so little is known about them. They may have been carried a long way from their original home and have often been mixed with spoons from a number of other regions.

BACKGROUND LACKING

Because of the lack of background information on so many of the collected spoons, it is impossible to say with certainty the part of Wales from which they came. An added difficulty to the problem of identifying spoons by region is that most are undated, which means there is no way to tell if they are an evolution of a local style or are simply copies of a particular spoon. In later years, professionals who had distinct personal styles carved many spoons. This further confuses regional identification as a prolific carver may have created many spoons in his style, and when collected without provenance his spoons could be mistakenly identified as examples of the production of several carvers working in a local style. A detailed survey of all spoons currently in museum and private collections might one day reveal regional styles and techniques, but to date this has not been undertaken.

In countries such as Sweden and Norway, spoons for museum collections appear to have been acquired with much more detailed information regarding their provenance, so it does seem possible to ascertain whether regional styles played a part in their lovespoon design.

An example of Dolphin Stem Spoons. (Photo courtesy National History Museum of Wales: St Fagans.)

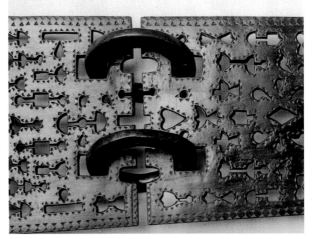

A double-panel spoon with rings. (Photo courtesy National History Museum of Wales: St Fagans.)

CHAPTER 3
Symbols and Decorations

It is in the area of lovespoon design and symbolism that the Welsh lovespoon is unique. No other country's lovespoons show the expansive and imaginative range of Welsh spoons. While the continental European carvers contented themselves with a few symbols, the Welsh embraced an enormous variety of them.

It has been suggested that a lovespoon can be read much like a book; that the symbols and engravings tell a story that the young woman receiving it would easily understand. This has resulted in a great deal of confusion, speculation, and argument among historians, carvers, and collectors. While there is no doubt that a large number of symbols are repeatedly found on historical examples of Welsh lovespoons, it is important to note that the variety of symbols was not as large as it is today. Ever since the modern revival of the Welsh lovespoon began in the early 1950s, new symbols have continually been added to the tradition. Many of the symbols now thought of as customary to traditional carving, such as the good-luck horseshoe or wedding bells, are not common to historic examples. The lack of written information and scholarly research on the subject of Welsh lovespoons has made them fertile ground for anecdotal supposition and it has become very difficult in many cases to sort fact from fiction.

In terms of technical skill, this spoon must surely rate as one of the finest carved. A masterpiece of Welsh virtuosity, awash in chain-links, balls in cages, and swivels, it is immaculately carved and represents almost unimaginable patience and tenacity. An elegant riposte to those historians who have suggested Welsh lovespoon carving was perhaps a less sophisticated cousin to the more refined European woodcarving tradition, this spoon exemplifies the fervor with which many Welsh carvers approached their spoon carving. (Photo courtesy National History Museum of Wales: St Fagans.)

Three categories

Dr. H.E. Roese suggests in his article *Lovespoons in Perspective* that Welsh lovespoon symbols can be classified in three categories: *Love* symbols, such as hearts and soul symbols; *Luck* symbols, such as horseshoes and the wheel of fortune; and *Fertility* symbols, such as vines and caged balls. This range of symbols is much wider than that found on continental European spoons.

Throughout the world, hearts are a symbol of love.

THE HEART

There is no doubt regarding the meaning of a heart carved onto a lovespoon, though: love.

The heart is a universal symbol, well known throughout Britain and Europe, and spoons were not the only romantic item upon which it was carved. Found in abundance on products ranging from stay-busks (used to give shape to women's dresses) to furniture, the heart is an unmistakable messenger of love. On a lovespoon, the heart was often given free rein and could appear singly or in profusion throughout the design.

A single heart was a message of love felt by the carver; twin hearts (especially if joined together) were said to signify mutual love. It has been suggested that a heart cut through the handle (fretted) indicated less passion than one carved from solid wood, because the skill required to do the former was much less than for the latter. I think it more likely the young men carved to their ability and the type of hearts they employed were more a reflection of their manual capabilities than of their ardor. Curiously, throughout Europe, the bowl of the spoon was seldom heart-shaped; this idea seems to be much more popular among modern carvers than it was in past days and very few historical examples exist in museum collections.

CHIP CARVING

Chip carving was a popular decorative feature on many Welsh and European spoons. In Wales, the chip-carved patterns tended to be fairly simple and repetitious and often appear as borders or simple fills to cover blank surfaces. In Europe, chip carving as bordering appeared commonly, but many spoons feature much more complicated patterns more in keeping with the work seen on larger ornamental gifts or on pieces of furniture.

Among traditional symbols, the origins and meanings of many are as mysterious as they are commonplace on the spoons. Several are positively mythic!

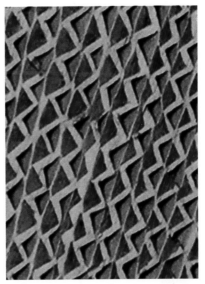

Close-up: Repetition of a simple chip-carved pattern results in a dramatic design which appears more complex than it is.

This spoon shows the broadening of the handle that was required as carvers became bolder with their ideas and increased the complexity of their designs. This spoon is particularly notable for its simple, but intense, chip carving, the unique heart-shaped piercing at the crown, and its beautifully proportioned and rendered bowl. Despite the spoon's large size, it still maintains a wonderful feeling of delicacy and balance. Detail from spoon handle at. (Photos courtesy National History Museum of Wales: St Fagans.)

SOUL SYMBOL

Probably the best known of these is the curious comma (or paisley) shape, which appears on many older spoons. The symbol is said to represent the soul and be Egyptian in origin. It is rumored to be a hieroglyphic symbol: a pictorial representation of the nostril, the portal through which the soul arrives at birth and departs at death. How an ancient Egyptian hieroglyphic symbol for the soul would have found its way to Wales and the rural carvers there is a complete mystery. Perhaps it was an idea brought by sailors voyaging to the Mediterranean or by their counterparts from abroad visiting Welsh ports. In any event, the actual Egyptian symbol for the soul (*Ka*) looks nothing like the Welsh comma shape, so it is extremely unlikely this lovespoon symbol originated in Egypt.

It is possible the symbol originated with the patterns on Paisley shawls made popular by soldiers returning home from India and the Middle East. However, spoons predating this fashion trend exist, which makes this a difficult theory to consider. Throughout Europe and the Eastern United States the comma symbol was commonly thought of as a "raindrop" and thus has a fertility or "source of plenty" aspect. The comma shape is also commonly seen in folk art as a wheel formation of four commas nearly touching at the center—a form featured frequently on Welsh spoons. It is conceivable that early carvers simply liked the shape. It would certainly have been easy to cut or carve and looks attractive when repeated throughout a design, so maybe there is a very simple answer to the question of its origin.

The diamond is easily carved, but a potent lovespoon symbol for a wish for prosperity. (Photo by Chris Roberts.)

This very simple broad-paneled spoon shows how a wonderfully romantic spoon could be created from an uncomplicated design. The spoon has a circular pattern and highlights four wonderfully mysterious soul symbols surrounded by hearts. The swan-neck stem is crudely carved, but the bowl is exquisite, despite some damage. Doubtless, this spoon was carved with very basic tools, but it still manages to exude elegance and make a strong romantic statement. (Photo courtesy National History Museum of Wales: St Fagans.)

DIAMOND SHAPE

The diamond shape appears often on historic spoons and is considered a wish for prosperity. As has been noted, the view of what constituted prosperity was considerably different among the rural folk of the seventeenth and eighteenth centuries to what it is now, and even the most modest expectations of today's courting couples would have been quite inconceivable back then.

Prosperity in those times would have probably meant enjoying enough to eat, having some warm clothing to wear, and being able to sleep in a dry shelter. The diamond shape, along with simple chip-carved patterns and some geometric designs, was probably initially included on the spoons because it could be easily executed with the simple tools available to the young carvers. By the nineteenth century, however, spoon carving had reached a much higher level of sophistication, and I believe it possible that this was when some symbols began to acquire meaning.

LINKS AND BALLS

The common whittler's tricks of carving chain link and making little wooden balls that roll inside a cage have also become the source of conjecture and disagreement among lovespoon historians and carvers. Some have suggested the number of chain links on a spoon indicated a desire to have children in a number equal to the quantity found on the spoon.

Even in an age when having a large family was expected and considered a very good thing, the large number of links found on many historical examples would have made a daunting proposition for a young girl. Several spoons sport a dozen or more links that would surely have been a most unappealing thought to all but the most extremely maternal. Many carvers now prefer to suggest the chain link symbolizes security offered by the suitor or that he is being held captive by his love for the girl. A number of carvers also read chain link as a good symbol for the ideas of loyalty and faithfulness; the couple figuratively bound together.

Similarly, the captive balls in cages are thought to be a light-hearted indication of the desire to have children.

This idea is more plausible, as only a very few historical spoons have more than a half dozen balls, and most limit themselves to two or three. The balls are also sometimes read as the man held captive by his love. Because chain link and captive spheres are common throughout the world in a number of carving disciplines, I tend to think

An example of chain link carved by the author. (Photo by Chris Roberts.)

This elegant spoon has a long thin stem containing several balls. A richly ornamental panel and a unique swivel crown the spoon. (Photo courtesy National History Museum of Wales: St Fagans.)

The etched line designs on this spoon are made more dramatic by the addition of colored sealing wax. The wedding spoon carvers of Brittany were particularly fond of elaborate wax inlay patterns. (Photos courtesy National History Museum of Wales: St Fagans.)

This rather curious large-paneled spoon is notable for a number of interesting features. Its most captivating feature is the ball in a series of three cages. Although not a particularly beautiful carving, it is very technically impressive and represents many hours of cautious labor. The broad panel, which would have had to be thinned down from much thicker stock, has been separated into three sections united by a series of four links. The link arrangement at the top was subject to a repair at some time, and it is extremely unlikely the link was arranged like this originally. It is far more likely the link was connected to the handle through the square central hole and not through the two heart-shaped holes. Carving the links as they are presented here, though possible, would be a mammoth task of great technical difficulty. This spoon had been painted previously and clumsily stripped, ruining the original patina completely.

they originated in lovespoon carving simply as a way for young men to display their talent and tenacity. Likely, as the lovespoon carving tradition evolved, meanings started to be ascribed to the techniques to give them even more cachet.

SAILORS' CONTRIBUTIONS

Sailors have had a profound influence on the development of lovespoon symbolism and were responsible for many of the symbols still found on spoons today. They added the anchor, a symbol of settling and security, to the spoon lexicon, as well as the ship's wheel and pictures of sailing vessels. Sailors whiled away the tedium of long hours at sea by carving lengths of chain, balls in cages (sometimes within a double or triple set of cages) and by engraving the spoons with pictures (in the manner of scrimshaw), which in one spectacular example are inlayed with colored sealing wax.

INLAY LIMITED

Surprisingly little inlay was done on lovespoons. A few examples exist where the carver has inlayed various incisions with red or black sealing wax, and there are some examples where a small frame is set into the spoon handle and a piece of glass inserted. Behind the glass would perhaps reside a lock of hair, or an inscription written on paper, and later examples may have held a photograph or a piece of mirror. There are few examples with marquetry patterns (inlaid pieces of wood) or with any other type of material, such as abalone or stone. The habit of inlaying was more popular among the spoon carvers of France and the southern European countries, who were fond of decorating their designs with colored sealing wax or shell inlays.

(Top right) Probably of Germanic origin, this extremely finely carved spoon illustrates a deeply religious theme, with a figure kneeling in prayer on the front face and a scene of instruments of passion on the backside of the bowl. The carving is of the highest quality with exceptional detailing on the basket finial and behind the kneeling figure. Religious themes rarely occur on lovespoons, which is surprising given the strong presence of the church in rural life during the latter years of the tradition. A lack of romantic symbolism would suggest this is not a lovespoon, but was perhaps carved for a more religious purpose.

(Bottom right) This wonderfully elegant little spoon is notable for the inlaid glass panel at the top of a thin, back-bent handle. Under the glass, a piece of paper has been personalized with a name, location, and date. The delicate bowl shows signs of having been damaged at the tip and it has been slightly squared during repair. (Photos courtesy National History Museum of Wales: St Fagans.)

RELIGIOUS SYMBOLS

Considering that many of the countries where lovespoon carving was popular were, and still are, very religious countries with church and chapel featuring prominently in everyday life, the scarcity of spoons that include the cross or religious symbolism as part of their design is most peculiar. Today, this is a common feature, especially on wedding-themed spoons, but religious symbols or sentiment seem to have rarely been highlighted on historical lovespoons.

HOME THEMES COMMON

It does not appear to have been unusual for several home-related themes to appear on Welsh spoon handles, though.

The key and keyhole appear frequently, symbolizing security, or more romantically, the key to one's heart. Small engravings of houses were sometimes etched onto the handle of the spoon, perhaps indicating the suitor's promise to provide shelter and security. Occasionally, domestic tools such as the spade or pick appeared as an indication the suitor was willing to work for his beloved.

MULTIPLE BOWLS

One of the more fascinating features found on many antique and modern lovespoons is the use of double or sometimes triple bowls. In Wales, a double-bowled spoon is thought to symbolize, *yr ydym ni ein dau yn un* or "we two are as one," the union of two souls joined as one. A triple-bowled spoon is often thought to indicate the wish for a child, the third mouth to feed. Although triple-bowled spoons are rarely carved today, the double spoon remains a popular choice for wedding spoons and for anniversary markers.

This spoon is an example of simplicity at its finest. Despite its plain appearance, it has been lovingly composed and has been created by a carver possessing the deftest of touches. The house, initials, date, and flower arrangement are subtle, but they are engraved with a sureness of touch. This spoon has been described as a wonderful example of naïve art, but there is very little naïve about it. The carver who made it was an assured craftsman (as is borne out by the exceptionally well-crafted bowl) who was also blessed with a keen eye for line, proportion, and balance. (Photo courtesy National History Museum of Wales: St Fagans.)

VINES, TREES, OR FOLIAGE

Vines, trees, or foliage appearing on the spoon indicate growth in the relationship. Many of today's carvers use foliage and flowers to indicate the passing of time (e.g., five flowers to indicate five years of marriage) and the growth and strengthening of relationships.

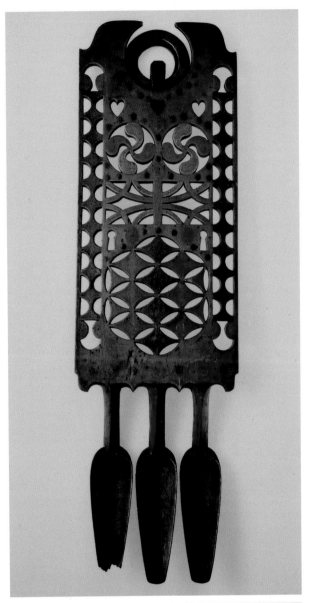

Vine, trees, and foliage patterns have long been a popular motif, both on Welsh lovespoons and on European carvings. Said to represent growth, fertility, and a long life, patterns such as these are very romantic statements. With the inclusion of birds in pairs, a message of love and coupling was also implied, possibly an allusion to lovebirds or the tendency of some birds to mate for life. Probably Swiss in origin, (where spoon and fork sets like this were popular tourist souvenirs at the beginning of the 1900s) this pair is wonderfully carved and carefully composed. Forks and even knives occasionally appeared as part of the design on historical spoons, and may have suggested the young carver would provide well for his love. (Photos courtesy National History Museum of Wales: St Fagans.)

Multi-bowled spoons were carved in both Wales and Sweden. Said to indicate the union of two souls joined as one, paired bowls were a popular symbol on spoons with especially wide panels. This very rare example has three bowls, perhaps implying the idea of having children together. Practically speaking, the carver may have included three bowls simply to balance the width of the spoon's beautifully pierced handle. The thoughtful and rather complicated handle pattern is completely symmetrical and as a further unusual touch, the spoon has been attentively painted. The elongated bowls on this spoon are immaculately carved, as is the single link at the spoon's crown, demonstrating intense pride in workmanship.

HUMOR

Some spoons had elements of humor in them, with the inclusion of features such as spectacles, which are thought to say, *I like what I see*, or *I'd like to see more*. Matrimonial jokespoons were also common to Sweden, where their humorously or outlandishly placed bowls created both a joke for the wedding couple and a rather surreal spoon.

LANTERNS, LAMPS

With the inclusion of a lamp or lantern in the design, there may have been an implied offer of security as a lamp was said to ward off evil spirits. Lamps, like spectacles were also thought to imply the notion, 'I like what I see,' or "I'd like to see more'.

BIRDS

Birds appear on many lovespoons from Wales and across Europe. When included in pairs, the intent seems to be romantic, indicating lovebirds and symbolizing pairing. When the birds appear singly, there may be more of a reference to domesticity and the notion of providing for the girl. Very occasionally, farm animals and carriages appear in the designs of Welsh spoons, but the only animal that seems to appear on continental European spoons is the bird (notably the chicken).

WHEELS

The wheel is an important symbol that occurs frequently in lovespoon designs. Whether as a ship's wheel, a wagon wheel, or just as an ornamented circle, the wheel shape may allude to the *wheel of life,* or to the notion of eternity. However, it may appear as often as it does simply because it was a relatively easy shape to draw out and can be impressively ornamented.

Though crudely carved, these "spectacles" make for a light-hearted lovespoon.

Here is another example of a thin handle. While the carving on this spoon is not extremely difficult technically, this lovespoon shows an increase in handle ornamentation and a subtle augmentation of the handle's size. A decorative finial carries a pierced flower pattern and the handle is vibrantly decorated with chip carving. A date and initial further personalize the spoon. (Photos courtesy National History Museum of Wales: St Fagans.)

FEW DATES

As noted earlier, dates are quite rare on historical examples, and although appearing much more frequently, initials do not occur with the regularity that would be expected with a romantic token such as the lovespoon. Low literacy levels may have been a contributing factor to the lack of dates and text on spoons.

TOPICAL THEMES

Toward the 1880s, topical themes began appearing in lovespoon designs. Particularly in Wales, references were frequently made to innovations such as the Menai Bridge, which connected mainland Wales to the island of Anglesey in 1826 and was considered a miraculous feat of engineering in its day. Royal events such as coronations or jubilees are occasionally commemorated and, infrequently, glass panels were inlayed to display small photographs, drawings, or text.

Occasionally, forks and knives would be carved, as well as complicated swivels or yokes. The knife and fork may have indicated the young man was capable of providing for the young woman. The swivel was most likely a way to demonstrate great technical skill and to show the woman and her family the young man's capabilities.

PAINTING RARE

Painting occurs only rarely on Welsh spoons, but is more frequently seen on Swedish and Norwegian spoons. When painting does occur, it is often carried out in bright, vibrant colors and tends to take a floral theme.

A beautifully painted Swedish feeler spoon is contrasted with two equally lovely unpainted spoons. Lovespoons are rarely painted, but when they are, the painting tends to be in bright, vibrant colors. (Photo Sören Hallgren © Nordiska Museet)

Kolrosing

The beautiful art of Kolrosing is common to Norwegian and Swedish spoon carving. This elegant and delicate form of surface decoration is achieved by engraving a series of light lines onto the wood's surface to form striking floral or geometric patterns. The shallow cuts are filled with finely ground coal dust or coffee grounds to give the appearance of colored inlay. (Photo courtesy of Judy Ritger.)

A curious thing

In several European areas, such as Sicily, the Südtirol region of Austria/Italy, and regions of France, small spoons with handles bearing the shapes of human beings were carved. Most often the character portrayed was dressed in local costume, however a type of Swedish bridal spoon features a nude female form portrayed quite realistically, but with the sexual organs as an exaggerated focal point. Although little is known about these types of figure spoons and the reasons behind their presentation to a bride or couple, there would seem to be a strong fertility aspect to them. (Drawings courtesy of Charles Western.)

'Traditional' symbols growing in number

Lovespoon carving is now virtually extinct in most of the European countries where it was once common. The only places where it is currently practiced in a meaningful way are Wales, and to a lesser extent, Brittany. In Wales, a myriad of symbols, which were once unknown or were very uncommon, have become standards since the revival of the craft in the twentieth century. Here, a myriad of symbols, which were once unknown or very uncommon, have become standards since the revival of the craft in the twentieth century. With each passing year, it seems new items are being added to the expanding list of "traditional" symbols.

Horseshoes are a traditional symbol of good luck, but their use on lovespoons is recent, as is the use of the lucky four-leaf clover. A horseshoe should always feature seven nails to be considered lucky and should be oriented with the open side pointing up so that the good luck cannot pour out.

Bells represent marriage, but like the cross, do not appear much on historical spoons. A popular symbol today, they are an ideal surface for engraving initials, names, or dates.

The barley-twist handle takes this notion a step further; like the double-bowled spoon it indicates the union and binding of the couple.

Nationalistic sentiment or identification can be shown with the use of the dragon, the Prince of Wales feathers (the badge of the Prince of Wales), the leek, or the daffodil, to denote Welsh pride. The shamrock identifies the Irish, the thistle the Scots, and the rose the English. A harp included in a lovespoon design often indicates Welsh or Irish heritage, but may be included without nationalist ties if a suggestion of musicality is being made.

Today, the lovespoon carver has access to more symbols, cultural traditions, and art styles than at any other time in history. Relationships and marriages now cross cultural, racial, religious, and sexual divides at a rate that would have been unimaginable in past times, all to the benefit of the lovespoon. Tradition is always changing, and the lovespoon is no different. Historically, it may have had a more limited set of symbols and been given in more restricted circumstances, but now it can be a much more encompassing offering.

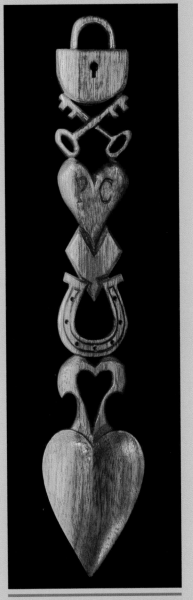

Symbolic Message, David Western, poplar, 2008. This simple lovespoon displays a mixture of old and "new" traditional symbols. 11" L by 2" W by ½" D. (Photo by Chris Roberts.)

CHAPTER 4
Interpreting Lovespoons

Although it is unlikely lovespoons were ever read like books, there would have been a great deal of romantic information found within even the simplest designs. While European lovespoons tended to limit design symbols and to be of a more conservative nature, the Welsh preferred a more freewheeling and effervescent approach. The diversity of designs, styles, and sizes found among historical Welsh spoon examples is unique in the lovespoon world. Not even the prolific Swedes came anywhere close to matching the variety found in Welsh lovespoon carving.

Outside of the commercial souvenir market, that imaginative and inventive tendency is still a driving force among many of the better lovespoon carvers working in Wales and around the world today.

Lovespoons are now presented on a range of occasions, with their meanings and messages tailored to fit each situation. As in the old days, many symbols are obvious to the casual viewer, while others are much more personal and even mysterious.

Natasha's Spoon (detail), David Western, maple. 17½" L by 7" W by 1" D. One of the goals of lovespoon carving is to create a design in which the various symbols have specific meaning to the recipient. The carver's first design challenge is to gain an intimate knowledge of the recipient's life or of the occasion the spoon celebrates.

Historical Example 1:

This piece is unique in having double bowls at one end and a single bowl at the other. Even more unusual, all three bowls show the type of damage that occurs when spoons hung on the wall fall directly to the floor, chipping the bowl tips off. Possibly, the spoon was displayed double-bowl end up and double end down at various points in its history. The squared ends were not originally a design feature, but rather the result of simple repairs when the bowls were damaged.

The comma shape is said to represent the soul. It may also be a fertility symbol linked to rain and the abundant harvest rain helps provide.

The heart is an almost universal symbol of love and passion, and that certainly would have been its message here.

The single bowl is a most unusual feature given the presence of the double bowl at the other end of the spoon. It may have been wish for children; the third mouth to feed. It is also possible it simply had no symbolic significance.

The inlaid frame probably once held a small piece of glass encasing a photograph, drawing, or love message. The framed picture appeared in the latter part of the nineteenth century and offered the carver an opportunity to further personalize the lovespoon.

The diamond shape suggests a wish for prosperity, the expectations of which would have been much more modest in those days and likely centered around simply having food to eat, clothes to wear, and a warm, dry shelter.

Wheels can represent the circle of life or be an indication the young man will work for his young woman. The circle is sometimes used to represent the notion of eternity, as a circle has no beginning or end.

Double bowl represents the union of the couple.

An unusual triple bowl spoon likely dating from the latter part of the nineteenth century. (Photo courtesy National History Museum of Wales: St Fagans)

Historical Example 2:

Certainly the work of a sailor, this spoon's nautical theme and the complex woodcarving techniques indicate a carver with a great deal of time on his hands created it. Because lovespoons are easily transported and require minimal storage space, tools, and work areas, they were an ideal medium through which lovesick sailors could express themselves.

Including a ship's anchor in the design is seen as a desire to settle down. Uncommon beyond the maritime spoons of sailors, the anchor is nevertheless a strong and easily understood symbol.

The functional whistle carved here is probably a display of talent rather than any sort of romantic statement. The entire spoon has a stronger, more masculine feel, seemingly substituting a display of carving virtuosity for overt sentimentality. However, there is a tenderness about this spoon's design and composition that is much more romantic than appears at first glance.

The knife and fork occasionally appear on lovespoons as an indication the carver is prepared to provide for his love. It is also likely that carving a knife and fork was a skill test that the carver set himself and may have been undertaken simply as a flight of fancy.

A very complex and elegantly carved lovespoon with a strong maritime feel to its design. (Photo courtesy National History Museum of Wales: St Fagans.)

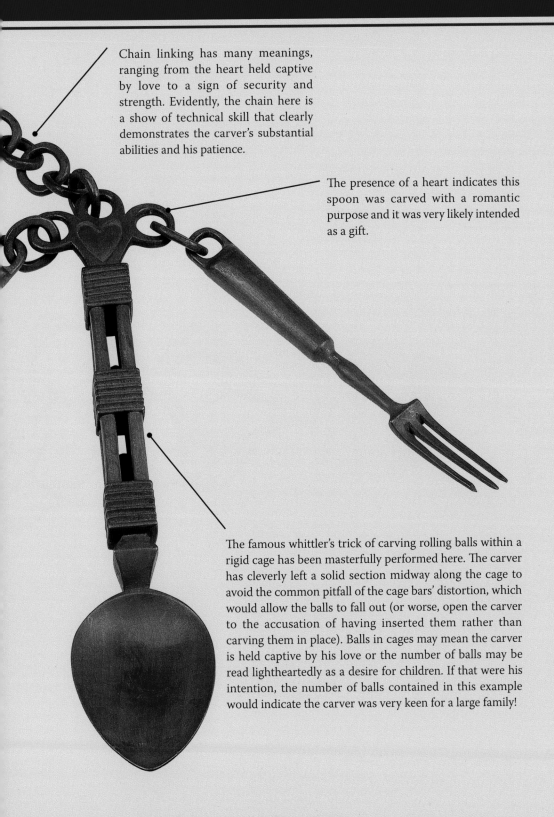

Chain linking has many meanings, ranging from the heart held captive by love to a sign of security and strength. Evidently, the chain here is a show of technical skill that clearly demonstrates the carver's substantial abilities and his patience.

The presence of a heart indicates this spoon was carved with a romantic purpose and it was very likely intended as a gift.

The famous whittler's trick of carving rolling balls within a rigid cage has been masterfully performed here. The carver has cleverly left a solid section midway along the cage to avoid the common pitfall of the cage bars' distortion, which would allow the balls to fall out (or worse, open the carver to the accusation of having inserted them rather than carving them in place). Balls in cages may mean the carver is held captive by his love or the number of balls may be read lightheartedly as a desire for children. If that were his intention, the number of balls contained in this example would indicate the carver was very keen for a large family!

Modern Lovespoon Example 1:
Engagement Spoon

It is rare in our modern era for a lovespoon to be given for its original purpose. Gifts to initiate relationships are uncommon now, but engagement presents are still popular. Even if the ubiquitous diamond ring does seem to be *de rigueur,* there is still a place for the wooden lovespoon.

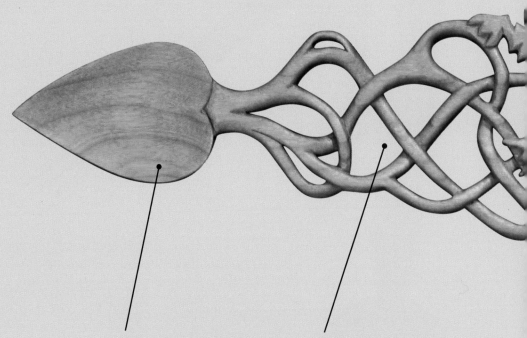

The heart-shaped bowl symbolizes love and unity. Heart-shaped bowls are surprisingly rare historically, but are elegant and beautiful ways to imply deep love.

Vines or foliage details are a traditional way to indicate both the growth of the relationship and the notion of fertility. In past times, having children was an expectation and fertility symbols were common to historic spoons.

Favorite flowers further individualize the design by personalizing it specifically to the couple's taste.

Twin hearts indicate mutual and united love. The addition of initials or names further personalizes that sentiment.

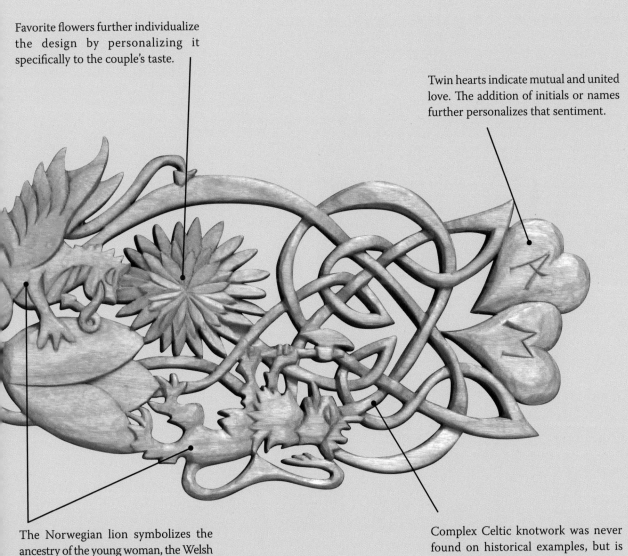

The Norwegian lion symbolizes the ancestry of the young woman, the Welsh dragon the ancestry of the young man.

Complex Celtic knotwork was never found on historical examples, but is now used both for its beauty and for the notion of eternity implied by the endless knots.

Caranza Engagement Spoon carved by the author from maple. The spoon measures 16" L by 3½" W by ¾" D.

Modern Lovespoon Example 2:
Valentine's Spoon

Valentine's Day and its Welsh counterpart, St. Dwynwen's Day, are days of love and romance and an ideal time for the gift of a lovespoon. The spoon need not be overly ornate, but it *does* need to be romantic. This is the occasion when simply designed but meaningful spoons along the lines of the Swedish *feeler* spoon are appropriate.

Hearts are the most significant symbol on a day like St. Valentine's. There is no ambiguity here; this spoon says *I love you*. In this particular design, the white hearts have been inlaid into the black walnut handle, leaving them proud of the handle's surface. Voluptuously rounded, they give the impression of white chocolates sitting on a bed of dark chocolate and are a reference to the standard Valentine's Day gift of a box of chocolates.

White Chocolate Hearts, black walnut with yellow cedar inlaid hearts, 2006. The spoon, carved by the author, measures 14" L by 3" W by ¾" D and is finished with Danish oil and beeswax.

Modern Lovespoon Example 3:
Wedding Spoon

Weddings are the most common occasion for the gift of a lovespoon in the modern era. Generally, the wedding spoon is the most personalized spoon and often displays initials, names, and dates in the design. Symbols of union and eternal love are also very common.

The wedding date is engraved into the design to commemorate the big day.

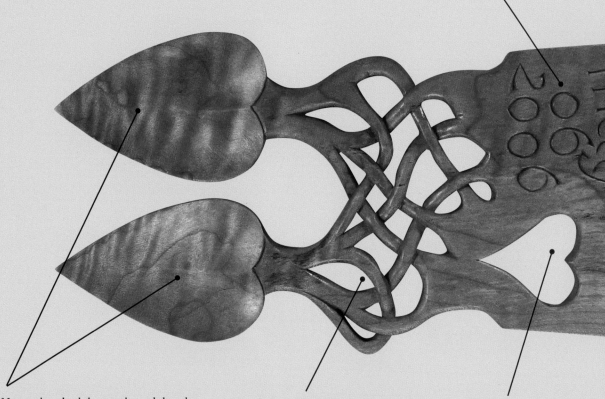

Here, the dual heart-shaped bowls represent a symbolic two becoming as one.

The vine theme indicates the growth of the relationship and of the family unit.

The large heart reinforces the message of love the spoon conveys on this special occasion.

An eternal circle symbolizes the wedding ring (which itself is an eternal circle) and surrounds an inlaid heart of olivewood from Italy, the groom's homeland.

A cheeky wedding saying lends a lighthearted touch to an otherwise serious design.

An endless Celtic knot is used as the crown of the spoon and is both a beautiful finale to the design and a symbol of eternity.

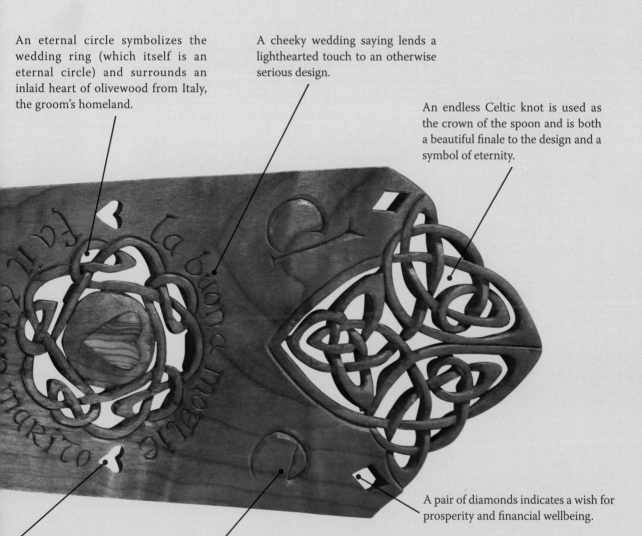

A pair of hearts indicates mutual love.

The wedding couple's initials personalize the spoon.

A pair of diamonds indicates a wish for prosperity and financial wellbeing.

Bertuccio Wedding Spoon, maple, 2006. The author carved this spoon, which measures 10" L by 5" W by ¾" D.

Modern Lovespoon Example 4:
Anniversary Spoon

After weddings, anniversaries are probably the next most common occasion where lovespoons are given, the fifth, or wood, anniversary being a particularly popular time. As with wedding spoons, anniversary spoons are generally personalized with names and dates more frequently than designs for other occasions.

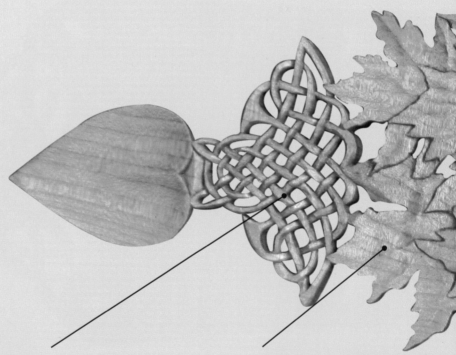

Celtic knotwork once again symbolizes both the notion of eternal love and the Scottish ancestry of the groom.

Maple leaves symbolize the couple's Canadian homeland and appear in pairs for romantic effect. If there had been more room, having twenty leaves in the design would have been a romantic way to indicate the twenty years of marriage.

The trio of hearts symbolizes love, while also creating a good area for the couple's initials and the date of the anniversary.

An Icelandic knot acknowledges the family ancestry of the bride.

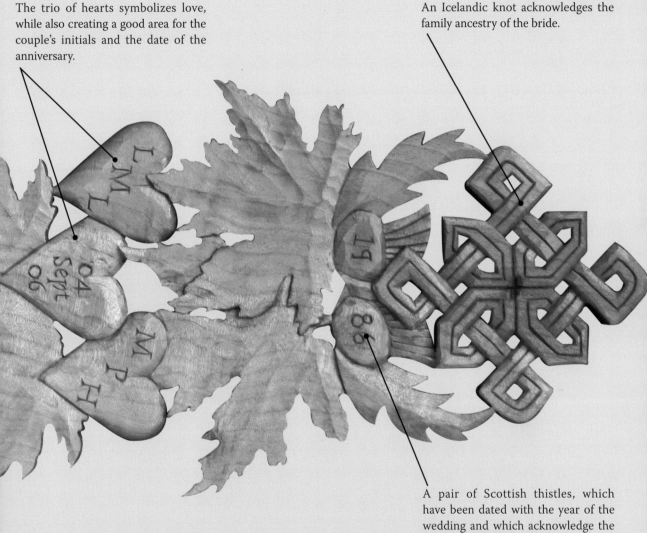

A pair of Scottish thistles, which have been dated with the year of the wedding and which acknowledge the family ancestry of the groom, support the knot.

Hennessy Anniversary Spoon, broadleaf maple, 2006. The spoon, carved by the author, pays homage to the Icelandic and Scottish heritages of the anniversary couple. Both Celtic and Icelandic knotwork features prominently in the design, as do Scottish thistles and Canadian maple leaves. Dated and initialed hearts further personalize the spoon.

Modern Lovespoon Example 5:
Birth/Christening Spoon

Although tradition suggests the gift of a silver spoon as appropriate at a birth, a lovespoon is a much warmer and more personal gift.

The angled bowl echoes children's feeding spoons once carved in Wales. Used in an age before high chairs, the angled bowl allowed a parent to feed the child while it sat in the parent's lap. The angle of the bowl allowed the spoon to be delivered to the child's mouth without the parent having to reach around too far.

The baby's parents have a great fondness for the ocean and it will play a large part in the child's life, so a marine theme forms the basis of this design. The dolphin is the playful mammal of the ocean and the one easiest for humans to relate to, so it carries the banner heralding the child's birth.

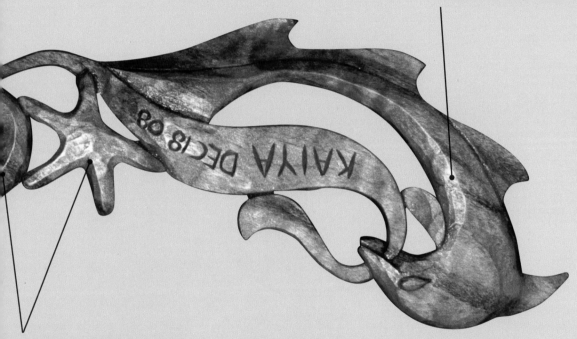

A collection of shells and starfish give the spoon its "seaside" feel, but are also playful and tactile.

Kaiya's Christening Spoon, spalted birch, 2008. Carved by the author, the spoon measures 8" L by 1½" W by ¾" D.

Modern Lovespoon Example 6:
Birthday Spoon

Although it is common in Wales to give a lovespoon as a present at eighteenth and twenty-first birthdays, the spoons are often better appreciated at later birthdays, when the recipient is more open to a symbolic and romantic gift.

A playful frog symbolizes one of the recipient's most prized possessions, a pair of gold frog earrings found in a thrift store for two dollars!

The heart-shaped bowl represents love, its raindrop shape a symbol of longevity.

Four hearts symbolize the recipient's immediate family members.

A tiny soul symbol makes a play on words (heart and soul) while representing the wonderfully vibrant soul of the recipient.

The 90th Birthday Spoon, maple, 2009. The spoon, carved by the author, measures 17" L by 5" W by ¾" D.

Twin magnolia flowers represent the recipient's daughters and their home state of Louisiana.

The hummingbird is the favorite bird of the recipient.

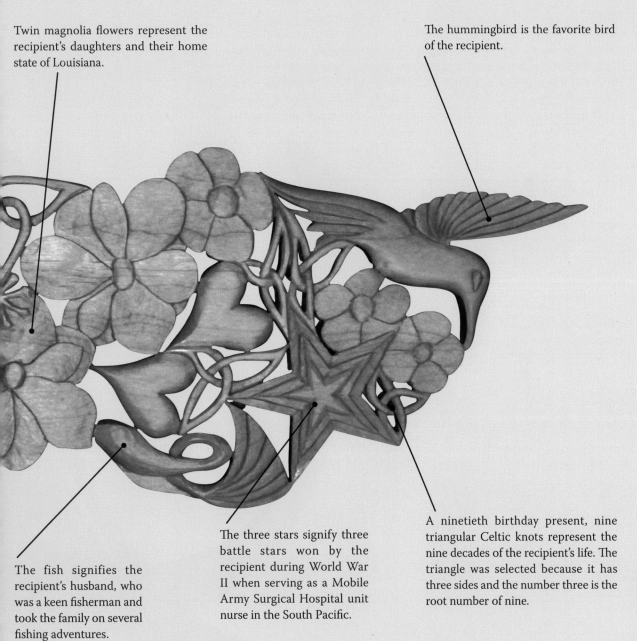

The fish signifies the recipient's husband, who was a keen fisherman and took the family on several fishing adventures.

The three stars signify three battle stars won by the recipient during World War II when serving as a Mobile Army Surgical Hospital unit nurse in the South Pacific.

A ninetieth birthday present, nine triangular Celtic knots represent the nine decades of the recipient's life. The triangle was selected because it has three sides and the number three is the root number of nine.

Modern Lovespoon Example 7:
Reunion Spoon

In the early days of lovespoon carving, the idea of a reunion spoon would have been pretty well inconceivable. That two people who had once had a relationship could reunite after twenty, thirty, or more years would have been made next to impossible by early death rates and a set of family and church standards that would have frowned on such events. Today it is not uncommon for high-school sweethearts to rediscover one another decades after going their separate ways. Often their rekindled romance is as passionate and intense as it was the first time around.

A heart-shaped bowl at each end of the design represents their love once again coming together and uniting.

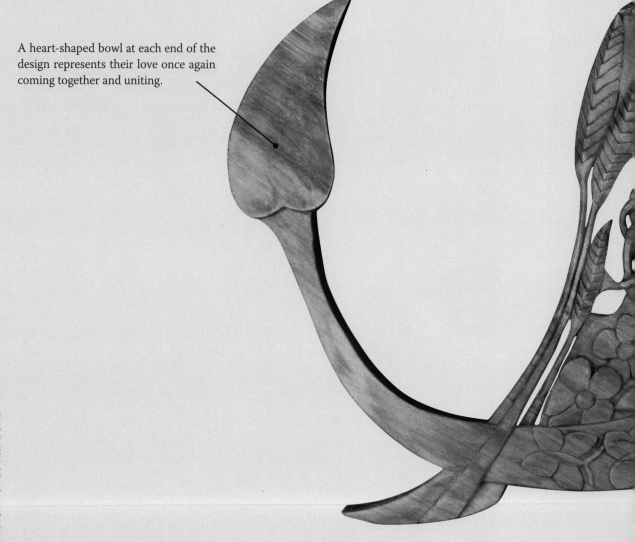

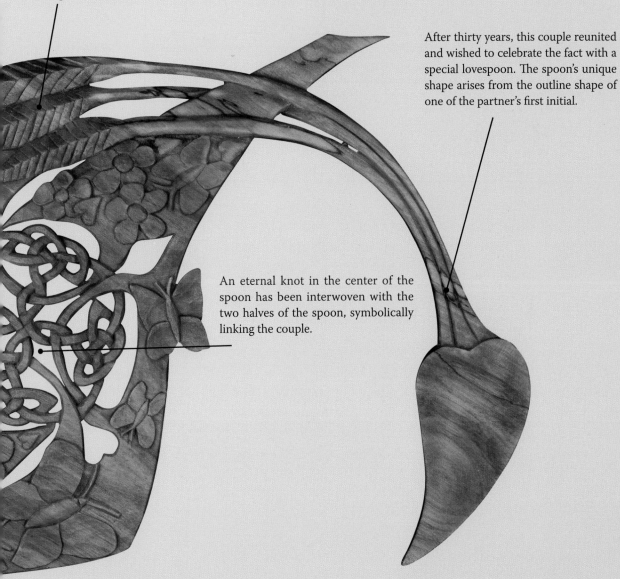

Because the couple was apart for three decades, the symbols for each partner are arranged in threes.

After thirty years, this couple reunited and wished to celebrate the fact with a special lovespoon. The spoon's unique shape arises from the outline shape of one of the partner's first initial.

An eternal knot in the center of the spoon has been interwoven with the two halves of the spoon, symbolically linking the couple.

A Joyful Reunion, maple, 2010. Carved by the author, the spoon measures 16" L by 7" W by 1" D.

Modern Lovespoon Example 8:
Celebration Spoon

Life is full of many happy occasions a lovespoon can commemorate in a lasting and beautiful fashion. This spoon, through a merging of Celtic and Islamic art styles, celebrates a safe return from the Iraqi war zone and is a fond gift from a father to his wife and family.

The double bowl symbolizes *Yr ydym ni ein dau yn un* or *we two are as one.*

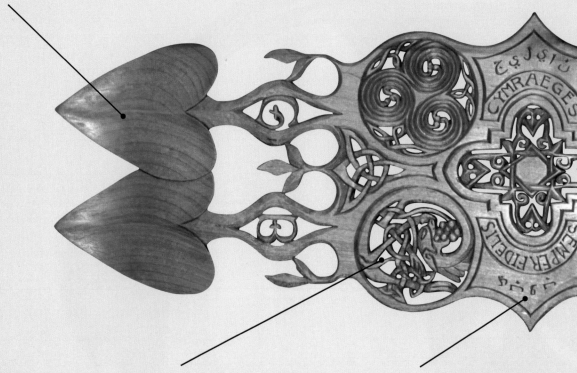

A small lozenge detailing their personal circumstances represents family members.

The parent's names are written in Arabic. Brief quotes in Welsh and English have deep meaning to the family.

IslamoCeltic Celebration, broadleaf maple, 2009. The spoon, carved by the author, measures 17" L by 5" W by ¾" D.

The Islamic patterns are taken from antiques in the family's collection.

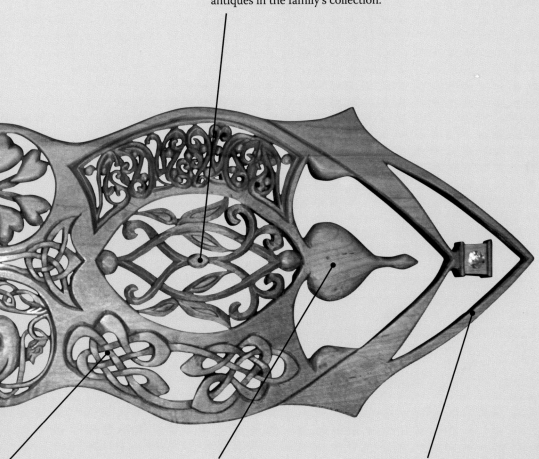

The Celtic knotwork is of the closed or endless knot variety to indicate eternal love.

A stylized dome echoes the mosque domes found throughout the Middle East and hints at the famous domes of the Taj Mahal, the very symbols of eternal love.

The crown of the spoon takes the form of a stylized representation of the Dubai clock tower, complete with an abalone shell inlaid clock face. The location is significant as the place the parents first met.

Modern Lovespoon Example 9:
Memorial Spoon

For those left behind, little can be done to dull the pain of death, but sometimes a lovespoon can offer a lasting, comforting, and heartfelt memorial in a manner difficult to otherwise achieve.

Although commissioned by a woman dying of cancer, this spoon, created for one of her best friends, radiates a wonderfully positive spirit and lightness of tone.

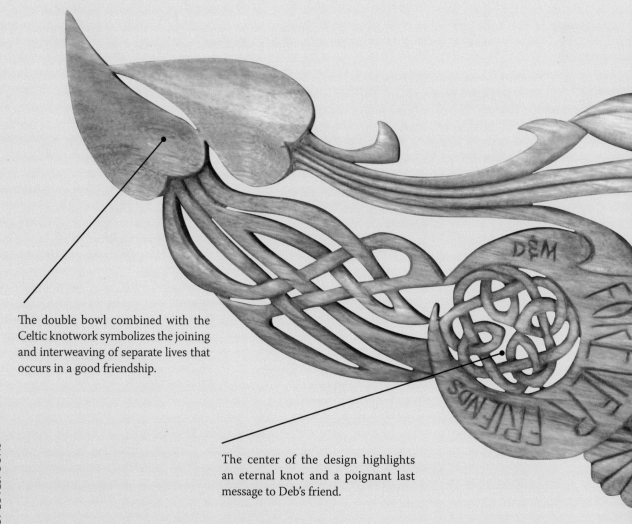

The double bowl combined with the Celtic knotwork symbolizes the joining and interweaving of separate lives that occurs in a good friendship.

The center of the design highlights an eternal knot and a poignant last message to Deb's friend.

A Message to Maryke, spalted birch, 2010. Carved by the author, the spoon measures 16" L by 6" W by 1" D.

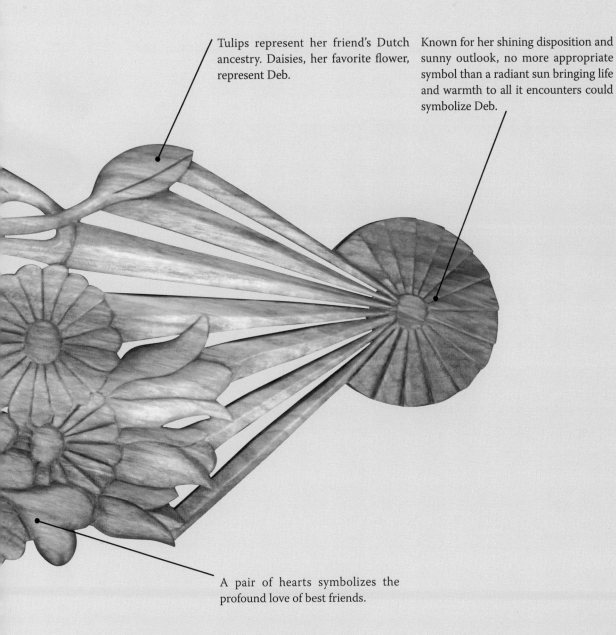

Tulips represent her friend's Dutch ancestry. Daisies, her favorite flower, represent Deb.

Known for her shining disposition and sunny outlook, no more appropriate symbol than a radiant sun bringing life and warmth to all it encounters could symbolize Deb.

A pair of hearts symbolizes the profound love of best friends.

Modern Lovespoon Example 10:
Presentation Spoon

The presentation spoon is a relatively recent phenomenon. Carved more as a token of respect or admiration than as a romantic gift, presentation spoons are often given at government, sporting, or commercial events.

This spoon traces the epic adventure of Taliesin, the sixth century poet and Welsh icon when, as a young boy named Gwion Bach, he swallowed a witch's magic potion and was blessed with ultimate power, beauty, and knowledge.

The baby was later rescued by Elffin, son of a great king, who renamed the boy Taliesin (fair brow) because of the child's unrivaled beauty. The baby grew to manhood and went on to greatness.

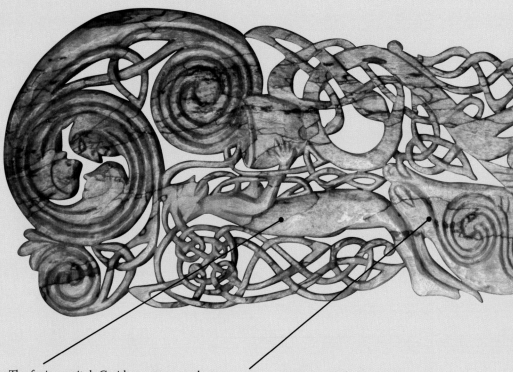

The furious witch Ceridwen attempted to kill the boy, but he fled in the guise of a hare.

By transforming into a greyhound, the witch nearly caught Gwion Bach, but he eluded her by diving into a stream and turning into a salmon.

Equally quickly she dove in after him and became an otter, but Gwion Bach leapt from the stream, transforming into a bird.

The witch swiftly became a hawk and seized Gwion Bach, who changed once more into a grain of wheat and fell to the ground.

Not to be outwitted, the witch turned into a fat hen and gobbled up the wheat.

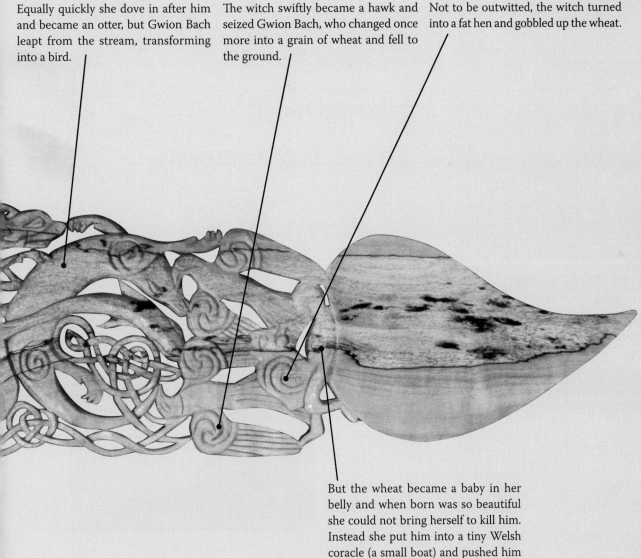

But the wheat became a baby in her belly and when born was so beautiful she could not bring herself to kill him. Instead she put him into a tiny Welsh coracle (a small boat) and pushed him out to sea to die by the elements.

The Legend of Taliesin, spalted maple, 2007. The spoon, carved by the author, measures 17" L by 5" W by ¾" D. (Photo by Chris Roberts.)

CHAPTER 5

Making a Lovespoon

Before the development of modern-day equipment, few tools were used to carve a lovespoon. A young man would have been lucky to have had an ax and a knife at his disposal and it was not until relatively recently that more sophisticated tools simplified the process and allowed carvers to attempt more complicated designs.

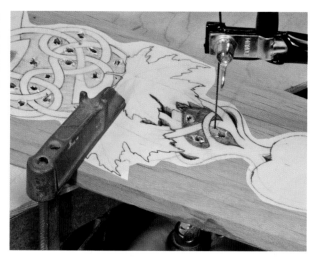

1 Today, tools such as jeweler's saws speed the shaping process. Power tools such as the band or scroll saw allow modern carvers to work at a pace that would have been inconceivable to the originators of lovespoon carving. (All step-by-step photos pages 72-74 by Chris Roberts.)

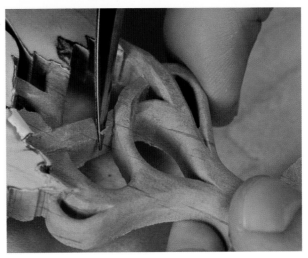

2 Intricate patterns, such as those found in Celtic knotwork, were once almost impossible to undertake, given the nature of the tools. Nevertheless, lovesick young carvers routinely achieved astonishing feats of craftsmanship and patience.

3 The knife has always been the workhorse tool of lovespoon carving. Most shaping and detail work can be undertaken with this versatile instrument. Coarse-bladed tools are used for the roughing out processes and finely tipped knives are utilized for the delicate shaping.

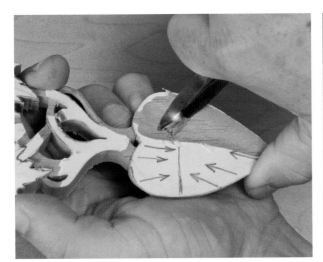

4 The bent-bladed knife is the one specialty tool that evolved for spoon carving. Used to shape spoon bowls and detail curved surfaces, the tool would most often be homemade, generally from a broken bucket handle or something similar. Many modern carvers prefer to use gouges to shape their bowls, but the bent knife is still versatile and reliable.

5 Achieving a smooth, beautiful surface is always a challenge. Historically, spoons were sanded with sharkskin, rubbed with knucklebones, or scraped with shards of glass. Modern abrasive papers have made the process much simpler and the results much more predictable.

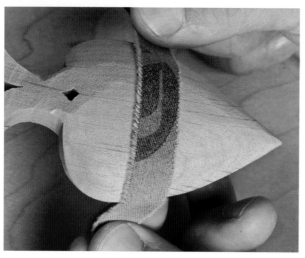

6 Well-crafted bowls are seldom found on modern mass-produced lovespoons. Historically, a great deal of effort was expended to achieve the elegant, beautiful bowl shapes, which indicate both a high level of craftsmanship and a good measure of tenacity.

7 The bent knife can come in handy for finishing any areas with convex or concave surfaces. Modern carvers may make use of gouges, which will work equally well.

8 The lovespoon has always been an exuberant thing, requiring a great deal of time and effort to be lavished on its myriad design details. Today, as in former times, a lovespoon is the physical embodiment of the maker's skill and the giver's devotion and it must always be of the finest work possible.

(Right) *Celtic Union,* red alder, 2007. Carved by the author, the spoon measures 12¾" L by 4½" W by ½" D. (Photo by Chris Roberts.)

9 Lovespoons profit from simple finishing. A small amount of penetrating oil or a few coats of beeswax polish are generally all that is required. Despite their fragility, most lovespoons improve in appearance the more they are handled. Many historical spoons have the rich patinas that can only result after centuries of contact by caressing hands. Where the spoons spent many years hanging above the fireplace or cooking stove, they have inevitably become darkened, with some developing a surface layer of tar from decades of exposure to coal smoke.

CHAPTER 6
Lovespoons Today—A Gallery

Contemporary lovespoons tend to be of two types. Whereas most are mass-produced for the souvenir or impulse gift market, a small number are still genuinely handmade by dedicated craftsmen. A recent revival has attracted a surge of carvers, whose creative, handmade efforts have often succeeded in developing the craft in inventive ways not possible in the commercial market. While many of the mass-produced spoons lack vitality, individuality, or style, a good number are very well thought out and crafted, representing exceptional value for their modest cost. Better quality mass-produced spoons often utilize highly sophisticated computer-controlled cutters to shape out intricate patterns that many old-time carvers would have difficulty rivaling.

Fortunately for those carvers who daily face down this relentless onslaught of technology, machine crafting has not yet caught up to hand skill. The computer does not yet have the imagination or emotion a human being brings to the craft, and it is often the slight inconsistencies the human hand leaves behind that gives a spoon special charm and character.

There are still many romantics, enthusiasts, and collectors who appreciate the skill and individuality of the hand-carved lovespoon and are prepared to make their own lovespoons or to seek out the craftsmen who keep this tradition alive. They know the craftsman can work to custom order, tailoring a design to be uniquely personal and deeply meaningful to the lovespoon's recipient and it is precisely this expression of emotion in the spoon's design that separates it from the souvenir.

Oak Cross, Garry oak, 2010. Commissioned by a clergyman's wife, this spoon carved by the author is a celebration of faith and the family. This very traditional spoon is composed of ecclesiastical motifs, such as the oak leaf and acorn, as well as traditional lovespoon symbols like the balls in the lantern, which denote two children.

As noted earlier, today it is rare for the lovespoon to be given for its original purpose. Very few couples begin their courtship with the gift of a lovespoon, and it is usually not until much later in the development of the relationship that a lovespoon might be given. Indeed, some have argued that there really are no "lovespoons" anymore and that most spoons could be classified as "gift" spoons or "presentation" spoons. Perhaps if we confine our definition to the original idea of a lovespoon, this is the case; however, any time a spoon is given with love or high esteem, be it at an engagement, wedding, anniversary, or simply as a gift, it *is* a lovespoon. If it is given or purchased merely as a souvenir or token, then it is a presentation spoon. Without that investment of emotion and passion, it is simply a decorated wooden spoon.

A quick glance at the Internet will bring up a multitude of machine-made lovespoon sites, but producers of handmade spoons are somewhat harder to track down. To illustrate the current state of affairs in lovespoon carving around the world, the following artists have been highlighted. They represent a diverse range of styles and techniques, with each having a unique vision of the lovespoon tradition.

ALUN DAVIES

Alun Davies is a master woodcarver of the highest order. An amateur in the very finest sense of the word, Alun carves for personal pleasure and never sells his work. His lovespoons are among the most finely crafted and designed spoons currently being carved and he has contributed a number of stunning innovations to the craft. His curved link chain, tapering, and offset ball in cages are *tours de force* of hand carving. Alun is also one of the best Celtic knot carvers; his gently domed knots appear so soft and ribbon-like that it is impossible to resist the urge to touch them. Flawlessly finished, every one of Alun's spoons has a radiant glow that gives brilliant warmth.

This collection of lovespoons by Alun Davies was carved from sycamore, acacia, and yew. The spoons measure 12" to 16" L by 1¼" to 3½" W by 1" to 1¾" D.

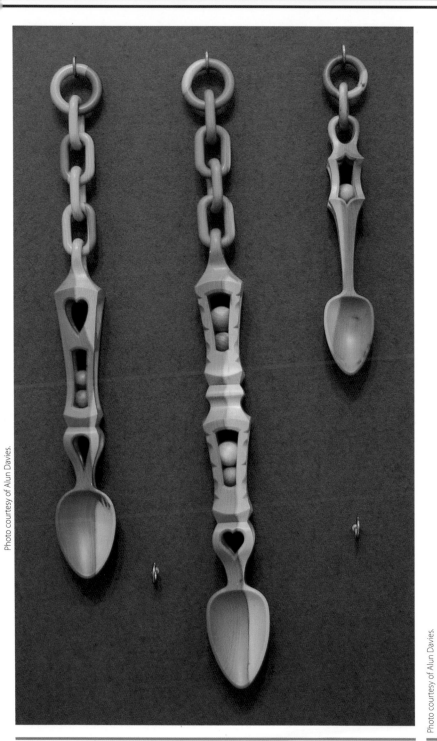

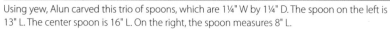

Using yew, Alun carved this trio of spoons, which are 1¼" W by 1¼" D. The spoon on the left is 13" L. The center spoon is 16" L. On the right, the spoon measures 8" L.

Carved from sycamore, this spoon is 12" L by 1¾" W by 1" D.

Photo courtesy of Alun Davies.

Photo courtesy of Alun Davies.

Photo courtesy of Alun Davies.

Photo courtesy of Alun Davies.

Measuring 16" L by 3 1/2" W by 1" D, this spoon is carved from sycamore.

HISTORY OF LOVESPOONS

Alun Davies used yew for this carving, which measures 16" L by 11 1/4" W by 1 1/4" D.

One of a series of six spoons carved for six grandchildren, each spoon with a different Celtic knot.

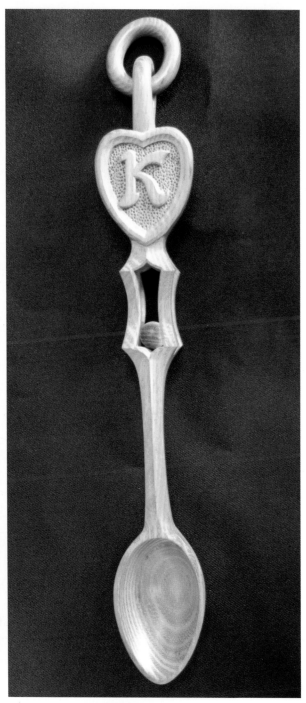

Spoon to celebrate the birth of a first grandchild (named Bethan) with a single ball in cage to represent the baby.

Spoon to celebrate the birth of Bethan's sister Katie, also with a ball in cage to represent the child.

MIKE DAVIES

Mike Davies is probably the best-known lovespoon carver currently working in Wales. A designer and artist, Mike has a keen eye for form and detail that is apparent in every spoon he creates. One of the first to expand on the craft's traditional roots by adding elements such as Celtic knotwork and sculptural forms, Mike's spoons are some of the most inventive being carved. His dramatic work is instantly recognizable, and he is especially adept at carving large, monumental spoons, richly ornamented with swirling foliage, complicated Celtic knotwork, and ornate chain work. Mike undertakes a great deal of commission work and counts both Her Majesty Queen Elizabeth and the late Queen Mother as recipients of his remarkable spoons.

Contact Mike at: *www.mike-lovespoons.co.uk*

Photo courtesy of Mike Davies.

This fish-themed lovespoon, carved from yew, measures 12" L by 3" W by 1" D.

Carved from lime (basswood) for Her Majesty Queen Elizabeth the Queen Mother, this lovespoon measures 20" L by 5" W by 1½" D. Mike Davies says he used lime wood because it is a gentle wood in appearance and delicate in color, which reflects the Queen Mother's character. The overall design is held together with a vine, leaves, and fruit, which symbolize a long and fruitful life. The vine has nine bunches of grapes, one for each decade, and each bunch contains ten grapes, totaling ninety grapes, one for each year of her life. The carving's two daffodils represent gentleness, growth, and the Queen Mother's association with Wales. The spoon has an ichthus, or fish shape, which symbolizes the Queen Mother's Christian faith. The spoon was presented to the Queen Mother during her official visit to Cardiff, Wales, in 1990.

Photo courtesy of Mike Davies.

A mother bird with her baby inspired this 12½" L by 3" W by 1½" ID lovespoon, which was carved in yew.

Finished with tinted polish, this dragon measures 24" L by 5" W by 1½" D. The carving was part of a theme exploration on dragons.

Finished with a tinted polish, this lime (basswood) lovespoon measures 13½" L by 4¾" W and 1½" D.

Using boxwood, Davies carved this fish-themed lovespoon, which measures 13½" L by 1¾" W by 1½" D.

A carving in sycamore, this piece measures 13" L by 2¼" W by 1½" D.

SIÔN LLEWELLYN

Siôn Llewellyn received training from Len Evans, a well-known lovespoon carver who was one of only a handful of carvers to keep the tradition alive during the early to middle part of the last century. Siôn's spoons are based in tradition, but his delicate Celtic knotwork and his deft handling of curved form give them a very contemporary feel. Working from a small, but efficiently equipped studio, Siôn carves his spoons from a variety of woods. His training as a cabinetmaker is evident in his skillful details, such as open barley twists or gothic framework around his knotwork. He is a master of chain link carving and like both Alun and Mike; he consistently carves beautifully formed bowls on his lovespoons, a trait that separates the best hand-craftsmen from the souvenir carvers.

Contact Siôn at: sionllewellyn@aol.com

Photo courtesy of Siôn Llewellyn.

On the left, a lovespoon carved from wild cherry. It measures 18" L by 2 ½" W by 1½" D. The spoon is finished with antique stain. On the right, finished in a walnut stain, is a walnut lovespoon measuring 20½" L by 4" W by 1" D.

A close-up of the Celtic knotwork in the photo at left.

Carved from holly and finished with antique stain, this lovespoon is 14" L by 2½" W by ¾" D.

More carvings from Siôn Llewellyn.

LAURA JENKINS GORUN

A self-taught American carver of Welsh ancestry, Laura Jenkins Gorun works from her studio in Ohio and has rapidly established a reputation for crafting exquisitely elegant spoons.

In Laura's words: "Research into my Welsh heritage in 2006 introduced me to the lovespoon tradition, which immediately captured my affection. When I began carving, I hadn't seen any lovespoons in person—just what I found on the Internet in a cursory search—so I had somewhat skewed ideas of what was 'typical' in design and scale. As a result, I seem to have developed an atypically delicate style out of this ignorance. I keep the delicate elements, though, because I enjoy the elegant look of them, and the challenge in carving them. It seems the fact that I am a girl comes through, even though I never meant it to do so. While my style may not look very traditional, it is the tradition itself that I love, and strive to honor. I suppose my spoons represent an evolution of the tradition."

Contact Laura at: *www.blakespa.com*

(Left) *Hyacinth*, housewarming spoon, mahogany, 16" L.
(Right) *Dragon*, lock and key spoon, cherry, 13" L.
(Photos pages 88 and 89 courtesy of Laura Jenkins Gorun.)

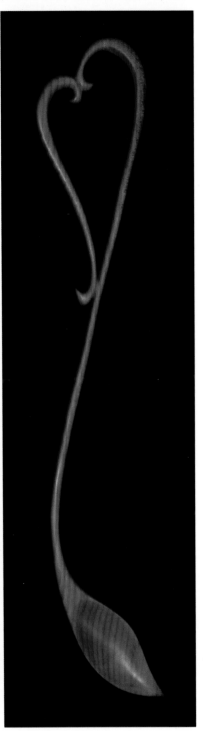

Double-Bowled Valentine's Spoon, English yew, 12" L, 2010.

Daffodil Spoon with Loose Link, lime, 12" L.

Simple Heart Spoon, English yew, 11" L.

DAVID STANLEY

A remarkably inventive Australian carver, David Stanley creates spoons that are a flawless blending of delightful design and meticulous craftsmanship.

David's gorgeously tactile creations are manifest representations of his vision of lovespoon carving. In David's words:

"To carve—by hand and with serious affection—a lovespoon from a single piece of thoughtfully selected timber, is to enter into a tradition that is obscure in its origin, esoteric in its existence, but also enthralling and winsome in its very nature and presence. We've had given to us for our cultural relationships, artistic intention, and a creative spirit, to craft as best we can, a gift for someone else, from what our own Creator has provided. Wonderful materials like timber will yield to the expectant and persevering use of our tools, an appearance of the hidden beauty of nature and of artifact, for everyone's praise and enjoyment of him. I aspire to the kind of work that looks as if it was produced in work sessions of pure joy, the natural result of well practiced hands and an experienced mind."

Contact David at: *www.whimsicalwood.com*

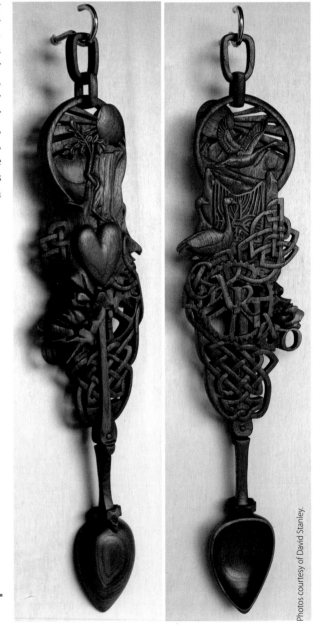

Cariad Lovespoon, European walnut, 16" L by 1⅛" D. Completed in September 2010.

Photos courtesy of David Stanley.

Photos courtesy of David Stanley.

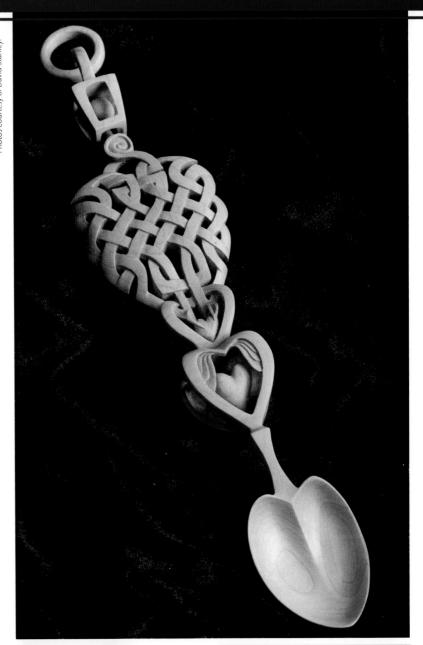

Celtic Hearts Lovespoon, rock maple, 12 ¾" L by 1" D. Completed in January 2010.

Lovespoon, English walnut, 14" L by 1.5" D. Completed in May 2007.

ADAM KING

Adam King grew up surrounded by traditional crafts and has been carving love spoons for the last 21 years. The son of noted rural craft authority Stuart King, Adam began using his first hand tools at age 6, and by the time he was 18, he had been demonstrating pole-lathe turning, besom making, and spoon carving at craft shows for many years. It was at this point that he realized he had a passion for carving lovespoons.

"My personal view is that lovespoons should tell a story about someone's life, either pictorially or symbolically. Often I will carve symbols of places people have met or visited and representations of things people treasure in their life. Combining these personal factors with more traditional symbolism creates a piece of art that can be treasured and become a family heirloom. As for the future, I have three small children, Isla, Elden, and Lilianna, to whom I hope to pass on my skills and knowledge so that this craft will continue flourish."

Contact Adam at: *www.adamking.co.uk*

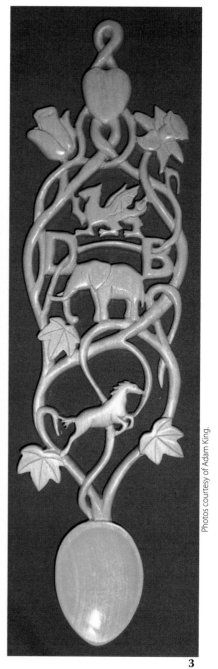

1

2

3

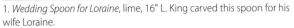

1. *Wedding Spoon for Loraine*, lime, 16" L. King carved this spoon for his wife Loraine.

2. *Welsh Daffodils, Vines, and Lovebirds,* lime, 10" L.

3. *Lovespoon for a Wedding in India*, lime, 11" L.

4. *The Celtic Tree of Life*.

5. *Celtic Knot Lovespoon*, 10" L. King carved this piece with a Welsh dragon facing a crow.

6. *Anniversary Lovespoon*, lime, 15" L. Each leaf on the carving represents one year of marriage.

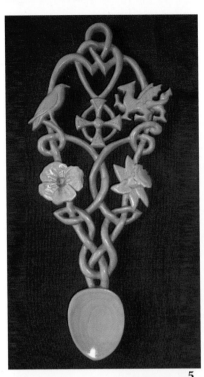

5

6

4

RALPH HENTALL

Ralph Hentall is known both for his marvelously detailed spoons and for his teaching and presenting skills. He receives commissions from around the world and has carved for former British Prime Minister Margaret Thatcher, the Archbishop of Canterbury, Rowan Williams, and Queen Sonja of Norway. In Ralph's words:

"I have had a passion for trees and wood since boyhood. In 1962 I read an article in the Woodworker magazine by Edward Pinto on lovespoons and the intricacies in carving them. Sadly, I had to learn the hard way, as the older generation of spoon makers had either retired or were dead. Curators of local, county, and national museums allowed me to study their collections and over the years, I acquired the knowledge and skills of my craft. My ambition is to pass my skills and knowledge on to others. To this end I teach practical spoon making from my home in Hertfordshire."

For My Wife Joan, sycamore, 1977. Carved as a present, the three loose seeds carved into the handle of the spoon depict seeds of fertility.

Photos courtesy of Ralph Hentall.

Thanking God for the Harvest, sycamore. The spoon depicts all aspects of the harvest—a reaper with his scythe in the cornfield, with sheaves of wheat ready for the flails, being blessed by the hand of Christ. The chain links a harvest mouse with a beggar girl sitting on a rock clutching a small loaf of bread. The girl is protected by all of the good luck symbols and faith—the trefoil, the dove of peace, the heart above her head, and the cross under her feet.

The Wedding of Prince Charles and Lady Diana, cherry. The top of the spoon has a crown with precious stones carved around it. It is joined to an anchor, symbolizing Charles' service in the navy, with a dual meaning that a man of Maritime Service was about to cast his anchor and settle down. Under the anchor is a panel with a picture of Peter Pan with a star (Tinker Bell) under his arm, which is meant to depict Diana's love of children. A link joins two crosses onto another panel with the Prince of Wales feathers. The stem of the spoon contains six loose seeds. A soul (comma) motif is above the bowl. Two smaller spoons are joined to the main spoon, symbolizing the couple's two eventual sons, William and Harry.

Wedding Spoon With White Ribbon, sycamore. A wedding gift for the carver's daughter and son-in-law on their wedding day in 1986.

DAVID WESTERN

A trained cabinetmaker and self-taught carver, David, the author of this book, was born in Cardiff, Wales, but now resides in Victoria, Canada. While running a cabinetmaking shop, a casual interest in lovespoon carving gradually became an overwhelming passion. David now carves lovespoons fulltime to commission order and teaches woodcarving at Camosun College in Victoria.

Specializing in complicated and delicate Celtic knotwork, David also draws from a wide range of art styles when creating his unique designs. Although he strives to advance the craft stylistically and technically, he keeps a foot firmly planted in tradition; all of his spoons are individually hand carved from single pieces of wood and all demonstrate the deep passion and commitment that separate lovespoons from souvenirs.

Contact David at: *www.davidwesternlovespoons.com*

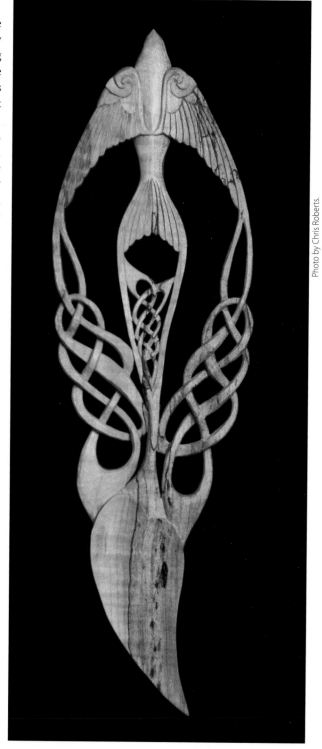

Flying Swallow, spalted maple, 14" L by 4" W by ¾" D, 2008.

Photos by Chris Roberts.

Stylized Heron, flamed maple, 6¾" L by 3¾" W by ½" D, 2008. Inspired by a heron feeding at water's edge, this very romantic spoon seeks to convey the elegance of the bird's form in a stylized manner, while hinting at tradition through the heart/love symbolism.

The Swallow, broadleaf maple, 15" L by 6" W by ¾" D, 2008. The bird hovers on the edge of the Celtic-style flower stem and stylistically between realism and the more abstract Celtic style.

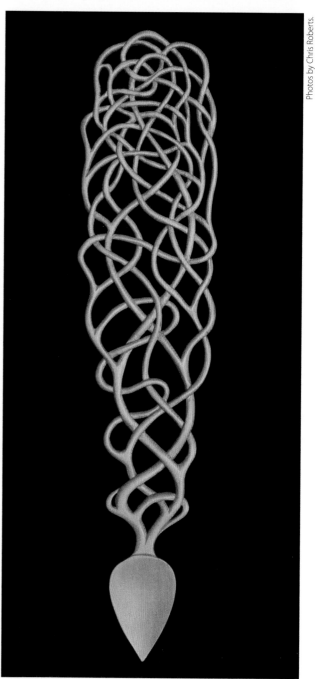

Photos by Chris Roberts.

Cym, red alder, 15½" L by 5" W by ¾" D, 2008. Lettering is often used on lovespoons to indicate initials, names, or significant dates. In homage to the style of Eric Gill, the English artist, stonecutter, and printmaker, the calligraphic letters here are supported by foliage rendered in a medieval style.

Vines, recycled old growth fir, 16½" L by 4½" W by ½" D, 2008. Despite the rigidity of the timber's straight grain figure, this design is an attempt to highlight the plasticity of the wood. The vine form creates great complexity from simple lines and has long been a lovespoons carver's symbol of growth, renewal, or fertility.

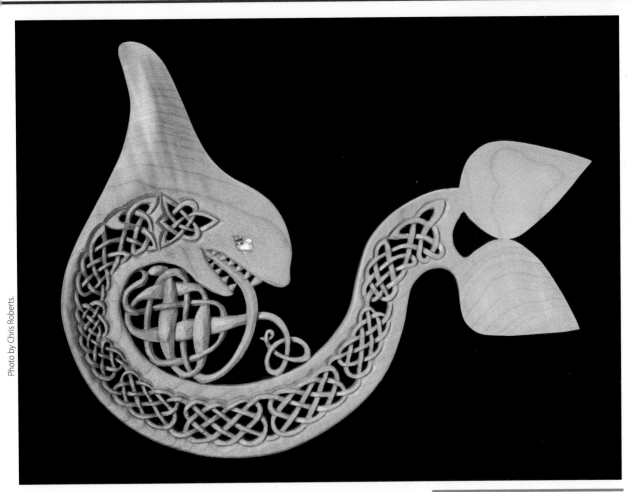

Orca, broadleaf maple, 11" L by 9" W by ¾" D, 2008. Themes of transformation combined with a masterful handling of abstraction and curved lines are common to both Celtic art and the indigenous art of the Northwest Coast of North America. This design pays tribute to both styles, while also acknowledging lovespoon tradition with the twin bowl tail. The double bowl has for centuries been a way by which the artist could indicate the joining of two hearts (or souls) into one.

Moon Over Newport, European walnut with yellow cedar inlay, 19" L by 5" W by 1" D, 2009. A moonlit evening when lifelong romantic vows were exchanged is the inspiration behind this design. The moonlight shines down into a valley where two souls are symbolically united by the flowing Celtic knotwork.

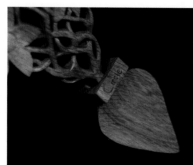

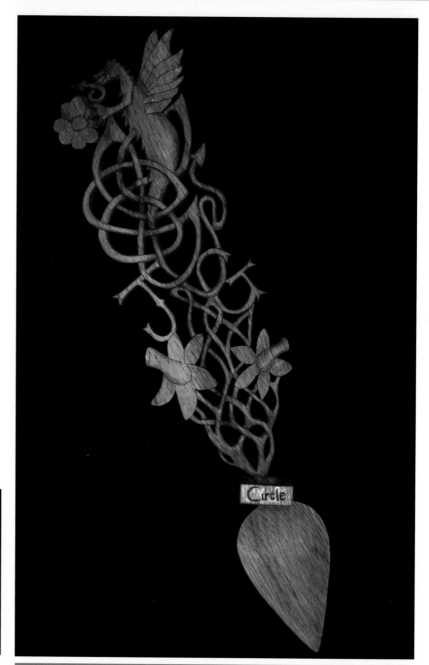

Jessica's Circle, Garry oak, 14" L by 3" W by 1¼" D, 2008. A short poem and an oak grove inspired the design of this wedding spoon. The square ring can be freely revolved on the stem of the vines with each of the four faces revealing a different word of the poem.

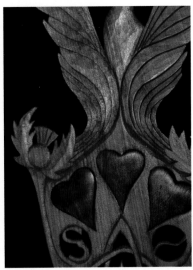

Phoenix Rising, broadleaf maple with black walnut inlay, 15" L by 4½" W by ¾" D, 2009. A celebration of triumph over adversity, this spoon depicts the phoenix rising from the ashes. Commissioned for a woman who had recently lost three family members, the spoon celebrates those lives in a positive and forward-looking manner.

Silver Fern, black walnut, 9" L by 4" W by ¾" D, 2008. In homage to the silver fern of New Zealand, this spoon combines elements of both Maori and Celtic design. The countries of Wales and New Zealand share many geographic and cultural similarities, not least a fondness for rugby, so this spoon was carved from black walnut as a tribute to New Zealand's mighty All Blacks rugby team.

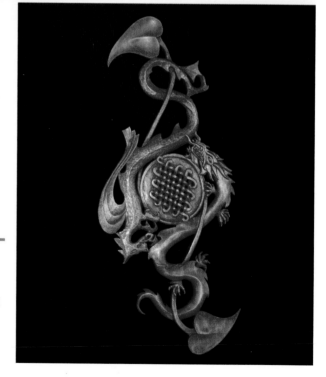

Dragon Knots, colored birch, 17" L by 6½" W by 1" D, 2010. This wedding spoon unites a Celtic-style dragon with a Chinese dragon. Circling around a Ming Dynasty central knot, the dragons symbolize strength, with the dual bowls symbolizing the unity of the couple. It is customary for brilliant red to be used at Chinese weddings because it is the color of good luck.

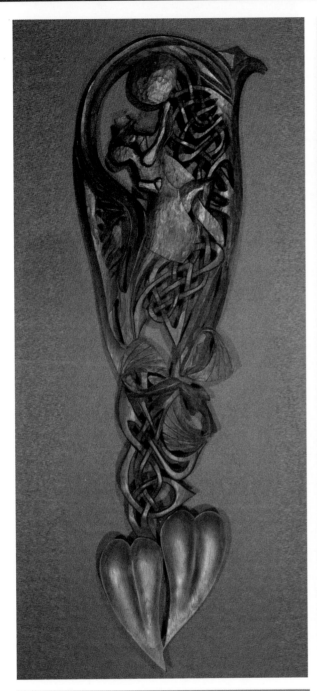

Tango, European walnut, 16" L by 4" W by ¾" D, 2009. A fiftieth anniversary celebration, this spoon shows the couple tangoing by moonlight. The three fish in the pool at their feet represent their three children. Leaves among the sinuous branches represent six grandchildren.

The Broken Road, broadleaf maple, 12" L by 2½" W by ¾" D, 2010. An anniversary spoon, the romantic imagery of the design is set off by a lovely little inlaid olivewood heart, which has been left proud of the spoon's surface and then lightly domed.

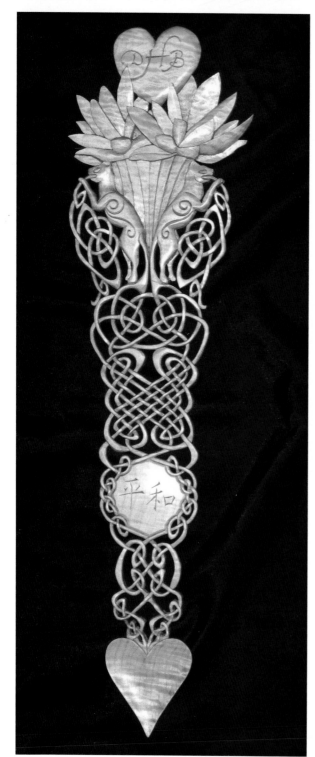

The Cats, figured broadleaf maple, 22" L by 7" W by 1¾" D, 2006. This wedding spoon utilizes lacy eternal Celtic knots to enfold a lozenge containing Japanese letters forming the word "peace." A pair of cats rendered in Celtic style supports a pair of lotus flowers, with a heart containing the couple's initials crowning the design.

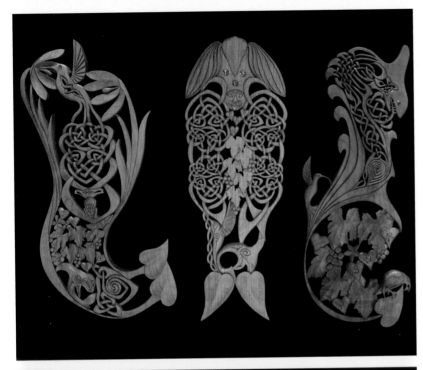

Trio, broadleaf maple, 17" L by 6" W by ¾"D (each spoon), 2010. Commissioned for three adult children by their father, these spoons act as a memorial for their mother, who has passed away. An animal character individually symbolizes each child, but all three are represented throughout each spoon design along with other symbolic details of significance to the family.

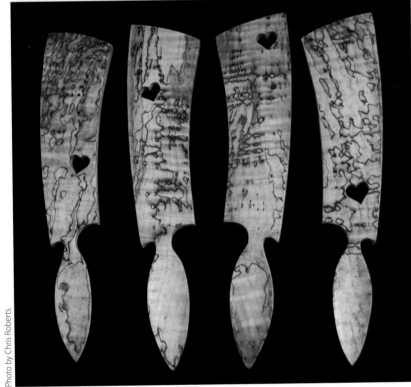

The Four Ladz, spalted broadleaf maple, 10" L by 3" W by ½" D, 2007. Sometimes the best thing a carver can do for a piece of wood is nothing or very little. This set of beautiful lovespoons has been split from the same thicker block with the stunning wood figure doing all the visual work.

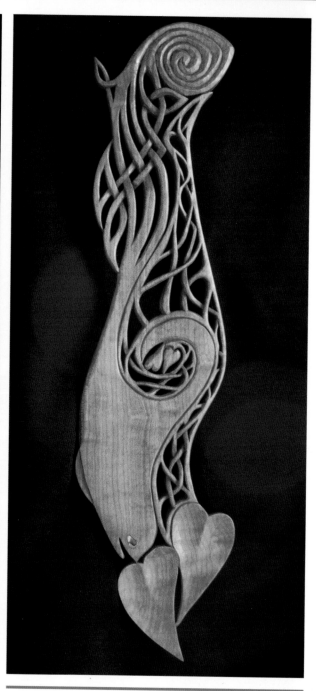

Hilary's Garden, broadleaf maple, 17" L by 6½" W by ¾" D, 2009. A rich garden of flowers and beloved family dogs share this design with a cascade of family members' initials. The rich grain of the broadleaf maple is shown to full effect in the sleek twin spoon bowls.

Diving Whale, broadleaf maple, 14" L by 4" W by ¾" D, 2009. This gift from parents to their son and his wife features a reference to the coast with the inclusion of a diving whale. The random nature of the "swirling water" knotwork contrasts nicely with the strict order of the Celtic knotwork, which flows into the whale's tail.

Birds, arbutus (madrona), 15" L by 5" W by 1" D, 2009. Another sculptural design, this spoon was commissioned by a client who envisioned a flock of birds exploding into flight.

Americymru Presentation Spoon, European walnut, 16" L by 5" W by 1" D, 2009. This spoon was carved for the Welsh/American networking group Americymru to be presented at their inaugural 2009 West Coast Eisteddfod. The spoon was donated as a fund-raising prize for this event, which celebrates Welsh culture in North America.

Photo courtesy of Richard Shick.

The Lost Spitfire, broadleaf maple, 15" L by 5" W by 1" D, 2009. An affectionate Christmas gift from a husband, this spoon celebrates his wife and their love for each other. Although this design is rich in personal details, the most poignant feature is the heart–rending swallow, symbolizing a great family sacrifice during the Battle of Britain.

A Royal Experience, walnut with abalone inlay, 2011. This stylized Welsh dragon was carved in celebration of the marriage of Prince William and Kate Middleton. Although the design is thoroughly modern (as befits the Royal couple), it is based on the classic Welsh broad-paneled lovespoon and retains a wonderfully traditional appearance.

Photo by Chris Roberts.

Detail from A Royal Experience: A three-corner knot symbolizing Prince William, Kate Middleton, and the subjects of the monarchy envelopes a "wedding ring" of laminated woods (symbolizing the many nations of the Commonwealth).

Sources

To see comprehensive collections of historical lovespoons, please visit these remarkable museums.

St. Fagans National History Museum (Wales)
St Fagans, Cardiff Wales CF5 6XB
www.museumswales.ac.uk

Ceredigion Museum
Coliseum Terrace Road Aberystwyth, Wales SY23 2AQ
www.ceredigion.gov.uk
museum@ceredigion.gov.uk

Skansen
Djurgardsslatten 49–51 Stockholm, Sweden
www.skansen.se
info@skansen.se

Nordiska Museet
Djurgårdsvägen 6-16
Box 27820
115 93 Stockholm
www.nordiskamuseet.se
Nordiska@nordiskamuseet.se

Norsk Folkemuseum
Museumsveien 10, Bygdøy
Oslo, Norway
post@norskfolkemuseum.no
www.norskfolkemuseum.no

Germanisches Nationalmuseum
Kartäusergasse 1
90402 Nuremberg
www.gnm.de

The very interesting and informative article, Lovespoons in Perspective, by Dr. Herbert E. Roese can be found at:
www.lovespoons.250x.com.